MW00618968

DEVELOPING YOUR
PROPHETIC
Filter

HOW TO PROCESS THE PROPHETIC

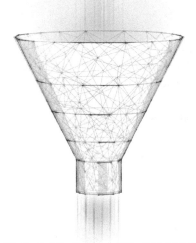

CHRIS REED

Developing Your Prophetic Filter: How to Process the Prophetic
by Chris Reed
Copyright © 2024

Distributed by MorningStar Publications, Inc.,
A division of MorningStar Fellowship Church
375 Star Light Drive, Fort Mill, SC 29715
www.MorningStarMinistries.org
1-800-542-0278

Printed in the United States of America
Cover design by Esther Eunjoo Jun
Layout design by Michael Fickess

ISBN—978-1-60708-005-3

For a free catalog of MorningStar Resources,
please call 1-800-542-0278

Acknowledgments

I am profoundly grateful to my wife, Missy, whose unwavering support and love anchor my life and work. Her strength and insight have been a constant source of inspiration throughout the journey of writing this book. To my family, whose encouragement and belief in my vision have been invaluable, I extend my heartfelt thanks.

I offer my deepest thanks to God for teaching me and giving me a voice to help equip this generation with the wisdom needed to navigate the path He has laid before us.

Special thanks go to Jeff Oliver for helping edit and format this book. His expertise and dedication have been instrumental in bringing the content to life.

To all who have contributed, in ways both big and small, to the creation of *Developing Your Prophetic Filter,* I am eternally appreciative.

Chris Reed

"BUT SOLID FOOD IS FOR THE MATURE, WHO BY CONSTANT USE HAVE TRAINED THEMSELVES TO DISTINGUISH GOOD FROM EVIL." - HEBREWS 5:14

Table of Contents

Foreword

BY BILL JOHNSON

In the DNA of every believer is the ability to hear and know the voice of God. Everything about your born-again nature is designed to perceive, recognize, and have fellowship with Him. We do so by living a life immersed in His presence—becoming familiar with His voice, His tone, His nature. Jesus put it this way: **"My sheep hear My voice" (John 10:27).**

Do you remember using radios? To listen to different stations, you could tune the radio either to AM or to FM. You could turn the dial across the whole AM band, picking up every possible station. However, no matter how hard you tried, you could not pick up something on the FM band. It's the wrong frequency. Similarly, the carnal man cannot receive the things of the Spirit. We need to be filled with the Spirit of God. Being filled with the Spirit gives us the ability to hear. Jesus said in Matthew 13:11, **"It has been given to you to know the mysteries of the kingdom of heaven."** The capacity to hear has already been given. When we purpose in our hearts to say "Yes" even before we hear Him speak, we are positioned to lean in and become hearers of God. He is looking for surrendered people who will live in anticipation of the One who speaks.

Our great privilege in this journey is to know God, and, in turn, reveal who He is to the world around us. In many ways, we do that by saying what He is saying. Jesus said in John 6:63, **"The words that I speak to you are Spirit, and they are life."** When we speak words that originate from the heart of a loving Father, life is released. The reality of His world is revealed. The disciples knew this well after spending time with Jesus, which is why Peter said, **"Lord, where would we go? No one but you gives revelation of eternal life" (see John 6:68 TPT).** In other words, Peter spoke for the group when he said, we don't understand everything you teach, all we know is we come alive inside when you speak. When you talk, we find out why we're alive. This is our responsibility as ambassadors of heaven: to become so in tune with His voice that we demonstrate the reality of another world and inspire a generation to hunger for the very thing we were designed for—heaven on earth.

Developing Your Prophetic Filter is an important book for our time. Prepare to be ignited as you read. Chris Reed lays a strong biblical foundation for functioning in a prophetic lifestyle. That, coupled with his passion to see the church walking in the things of God, creates an impactful resource that will not only equip the readers to learn to prophesy, but also invite each of us to truly become vessels God desires to use. May we be a people who walk in purity, passion, and power, representing Jesus well through the gift of prophecy.

Bill Johnson
Bethel Church, Redding, CA
Author of ***Open Heavens*** and ***Born for Significance***

PREPARING FOR
the Prophetic

What is "the prophetic"? It's been said that God speaks much less than many claim but much more than many hear. One of the most important qualities a Christian can develop is the discipline of hearing, processing, and applying God's voice to their life. God's Word is clear: God desires to communicate with His children.

He not only desires to speak to apostles, prophets, and pastors, but He also wants to reveal Himself and His Word to every believer who desires to hear what He is saying at any moment. We know the Bible is the inspired, infallible, written Word of God. All we need to experience salvation and successfully walk with God can be found in the Holy Bible, and nothing God speaks to us personally should ever contradict the Bible.

"But He answered and said, "It is written, 'Man shall not live by bread alone, but by every word that proceeds from the mouth of God'" (Matthew 4:4). One keyword in this Scripture is **"proceeds."** This implies that, just as man requires a "process" or a "proceeding" of daily bread for physical sustenance, he also requires a "process" or a "proceeding" of words from God for spiritual sustenance.

"Who then is a faithful and wise servant, whom his master made ruler over his household, to give them food in due season?" (Matthew 24:45) Jesus described a **"faithful and wise servant"** as someone who rules His house well by regularly providing spiritual food in a timely manner. There is no greater mandate for leadership in God's church than to deliver to God's people what God is saying in a timely fashion and according to what they need to hear at a given moment. This is the **"word that proceeds"** spoken of in Matthew 4:4. Whatever God is saying to His people to bring guidance, instruction, or perspective is spiritual **"food in due season."**

For us to be deemed faithful and wise servants and fulfill this charge, we must provide the word that proceeds for the church so they can receive, apply, and appropriate these words to their lives. To do so, there must be people who have learned how to both hear and correctly interpret what God is saying.

There is nothing more important for the body of Christ in this hour than to have equippers and trainers who can teach God's people how to hear, interpret, and apply God's voice in the appropriate settings. This can only happen when we take time to learn everything we can about hearing and sharing God's voice. This is the simplest and most accurate definition of prophetic gifts. "The prophetic" is all about learning to hear God's voice for ourselves and others, and knowing if we should share it, and who we should share it with, in a timely manner.

SOME SAID "IT THUNDERED"

Now My soul is troubled, and what shall I say? "Father, save Me from this hour'? But for this purpose I came to this hour. Father, glorify Your name.

Then a voice came from heaven, saying, "I have both glorified it and will glorify it again."

Therefore the people who stood by and heard it said that it had thundered. Others said, "An angel has spoken to Him."

Jesus answered and said, "This voice did not come because of Me, but for your sake. Now is the judgment of this world; now the ruler of this world will be cast out" (John 12:27-31).

In this New Testament example of God speaking from heaven, we can identify at least three different groups of people, each of whom heard God's voice to varying degrees.

1.   Some said that "it had thundered."
2.   Others said, "An angel has spoken."
3.   Jesus said, "This voice has not come because of Me, but for your sake."

This is a perfect example of what happens in many churches and Christian circles when God speaks. Three different groups of people heard the same voice from heaven at the same time and in the same location, yet each heard something different. The first group heard the voice of God the Father. They said, "it sounded like thunder." They did not hear *what* was said or *why*; all they heard was a thundering sound with no real meaning.

The second group heard the same sound but differently. Whatever they heard, they concluded it was an angel that had spoken to Jesus. Clearly, they knew something supernatural had happened, but they could not determine the origin of the voice or to whom it spoke. They thought it was the voice of an angel, when in reality it was the voice of God.

The third group (usually the smallest group) hears, interprets, and applies correctly what was said. In this example, Jesus alone represented this third group. Jesus clarified this was more than just "thunder," as some said. He also clarified this voice was not of angelic origin. Finally, He clarified the voice was not for His sake, but for the sake of the people.

This example of three groups of people listening to the same voice but hearing three different things is common. Often, people know they heard "something" but cannot define it. Others know it was supernatural but don't know the origin of the message or to whom it was spoken. Jesus was the perfect example of a prophetic leader. He knew the voice of His Father. He even said, **"All things that I heard from My Father I have made known unto you" (see John 15:15).** And **"I can of Myself do nothing. As I hear, I judge; and My judgment is righteous, because I do not seek My own will but the will of the Father who sent Me" (John 5:30).**

How often do we hurry through life with our minds focused on the physical realm through our five senses? Yet, when we slow down, reflect on the issues and events of the day, and quiet our "brain chatter," we realize God has been trying to speak to us. Brain chatter can be the biggest hindrance to hearing and discerning God's voice. How many times has the "rat race" of our lives drowned out God's voice? I can look back on many times in my life when I realized I was not as perceptive to the spirit realm because I was overly perceptive to the physical realm.

GOD WANTS TO SPEAK TO US

Everything changes though when we realize God wants to speak to us regularly. He wants to speak His love, direction, and understanding into our lives. The three groups represented in

John 12:28 all knew there was a sound from heaven, but most were dull of hearing. All three groups were sensitive enough to realize they were receiving "a word," but many were unsure who the word was for or if they should even share it.

Now, more than ever, as the body of Christ, we must learn to hear, interpret, and apply God's voice collectively. In some religious groups, the leaders don't want the people to learn to hear from God for themselves. Perhaps they fear the people will not look to them to hear God's voice and they'll be out of a job. Yet, even if everyone *did* hear from God, this would not negate the need for spiritual leadership. In fact, the very purpose of New Testament leadership is to train and equip the saints, so they *can* hear from God and do the work of the ministry.

We must see the value of having more than one or two people in our church with a track record of hearing clearly from God. Instead, we need an entire *company* of people who will prioritize the necessary training and equipping to properly discern God's voice. We must have our senses matured to the point that we can *all* perceive God's voice when He speaks and not act on it until we have clarity.

DISTINGUISHING THE SPIRITUAL FROM THE NATURAL

There is no greater mandate for believers than to learn to identify the witness of the Spirit's voice and to discern and judge correctly. How can we effectively fulfill the Great Commission without hearing God's voice? We must train our spiritual senses to perceive what is happening in the spirit realm, while simultaneously receiving information with our physical senses in our daily lives and experiences. 1 Corinthians 2:9-16 explains the process of distinguishing natural and spiritual information simultaneously.

But as it is written:

"Eye has not seen, nor ear heard, nor have entered into the heart of man the things which God has prepared for those who love Him."

But God has revealed them to us through His Spirit. For the Spirit searches all things, yes, the deep things of God. For what man knows the things of a man except the spirit of the man which is in him? Even so no one knows the things of God except the Spirit of God. Now we have received, not the spirit of the world, but the Spirit who is from God, that we might know the things that have been freely given to us by God.

These things we also speak, not in words which man's wisdom teaches but which the Holy Spirit teaches, comparing spiritual things with spiritual. But the natural man does not receive the things of the Spirit of God, for they are foolishness to him; nor can he know them, because they are spiritually discerned. But he who is spiritual judges all things, yet he himself is rightly judged by no one. For "who has known the mind of the Lord that he may instruct Him?" But we have the mind of Christ.

Since we are spiritual people living in a physical world, we must be able to "judge" whether our day-to-day experiences are physical experiences with spiritual meanings or just plain physical experiences. Remember, we are not physical beings with spiritual experiences; we are first spiritual beings with physical experiences.

PROPHECY: A GIFT FOR ALL BELIEVERS

Prophecy is not a gift for leaders only. It is a gift which Paul said *all* Christians should pursue. He even told us that speaking

14

in other tongues as the Holy Spirit gives us utterance was for personal edification—unless an interpreter was present so others could understand. In contrast, prophecy is about learning to hear from God and sharing His voice with others when appropriate, depending on whether the word is for, to, or about them.

> **Pursue love, and desire spiritual gifts, but especially that you may prophesy. For he who speaks in a tongue does not speak to men but to God, for no one understands him; however, in the spirit he speaks mysteries. But he who prophesies speaks edification and exhortation and comfort to men. He who speaks in a tongue edifies himself, but he who prophesies edifies the church. I wish you all spoke with tongues, but even more that you prophesied; for he who prophesies is greater than he who speaks with tongues, unless indeed he interprets, that the church may receive edification (1 Corinthians 14:1-5).**

The purpose of the gifts of the Spirit are to edify *all* believers. When we understand that God desires to speak to *all*, not just some, this will awaken in us a desire to learn His language and process the prophetic.

KNOWING HIS VOICE

Jimmy Swaggart wrote a song called "His Voice Makes the Difference." Here are the lyrics:

His voice makes the difference
When He speaks, He relieves my troubled mind
It's the only voice I hear that makes the difference
And I'll follow one day at a time

When I need Him, I know where to find Him
In my place of prayer, His Spirit hovers near

His voice gently gives me my direction
And I'll follow that voice that I hear

His voice is a strong and a mighty tower
Tearing down every stronghold in my life
He's the master of the wind and the storm that rages
When He speaks, all my darkness turns to light

Hearing and knowing God's voice is what the prophetic is all about. Jesus said, **"I can of Myself do nothing" (see John 5:30),** only what He hears from the Father. True prophets wait, then hear, then finally speak. We must know His voice. Speaking before or without hearing Him is presumption. Without the backup of heaven, we are in dangerous territory.

> **"Truly, truly, I say to you, he who does not enter by the door into the fold of the sheep, but climbs up some other way, he is a thief and a robber. But he who enters by the door is a shepherd of the sheep. To him the doorkeeper opens, and the sheep hear his voice, and he calls his own sheep by name and leads them out. When he puts forth all his own, he goes ahead of them, and the sheep follow him because they know his voice. A stranger they simply will not follow, but will flee from him, because they do not know the voice of strangers" (John 10:1-5 NASB).**

If it takes being a sheep to hear God's voice, I'm all in! Jesus said in John 10:14, **"I am the good shepherd; and I know My sheep, and am known by My own."** In the Old Testament, they saw God as indivisibly one God, but they also spoke of the Holy Spirit. The Holy Spirit rested on the prophets when they spoke. In Genesis 1:2, **"the Spirit of God was hovering over the face of the waters."** The Spirit of God and the voice of God were one and the same. Likewise, in the New Testament, we must know

God's voice, the voice of the Spirit. We can hear, taste, and smell the Spirit.

In John 10, Jesus spoke metaphorically using imagery of "sheep," a "shepherd," and "robbers." He also spoke of a "gate" and a "door." The gatekeeper for Jesus was John the Baptist. He opened the door for all of us when he baptized Jesus saying, **"Behold! The Lamb of God who takes away the sin of the world!" (see John 1:29).** However, the Holy Spirit is the ultimate gatekeeper who opens the door for us to hear the voice of the Good Shepherd. Not only can the super-spiritual, religious, elite, pastors, teachers, and apostles hear God's voice, Jesus said, **"My *sheep* hear My voice" (see John 10:27,** emphasis added).

We don't need to be pastors or great leaders to hear God's voice. *Sheep* means all of us. If you're a "sheep," you *will* hear God's voice. This is not an exclusive club. If you believe God speaks, you can also believe to hear God's voice. God speaks to His sheep, and He will leave the ninety-nine to reach the one (see Matthew 18:12-14). When you realize that He speaks personally to us and does not abandon us, you can begin to take ownership and expect God to speak to you.

THE SPIRIT OF GOD IS THE VOICE OF GOD

"I have many more things to say to you, but you cannot bear them now. But when He, the Spirit of truth, comes, He will guide you into all the truth; for He will not speak on His own initiative, but whatever He hears, He will speak; and He will disclose to you what is to come. He will glorify Me, for He will take of Mine and will disclose it to you. All things that the Father has are Mine; therefore I said that He takes of Mine and will disclose it to you" (John 16:12-15 NASB).

Jesus said this on the night He was arrested and just before His trial and crucifixion. At the Last Supper, Jesus gave them His last will and testament. He had three-and-a-half years to speak to them, then He said, "I still have more to tell you." The disciples heard Him speak to the crowds and then to them personally. They watched Him go to the mountain and pray. Jesus said the Holy Spirit would teach us **"all things"** and help us understand everything He had to say (see John 14:26). The disciples listened intently to Jesus at the Last Supper, but Jesus knew it was not the right time to share everything. The solution was for the Spirit of truth to later come to us, steer us toward the truth, and reveal to us what we need to know.

The spirit of prophecy is the testimony of Jesus (see Revelation 19:10). Jesus said the Holy Spirit would reveal who He was and why He came. It took a step of faith for the disciples to start listening to the Holy Spirit because, until then, they had only learned by listening to Jesus. Jesus said we would know His voice better today by listening to the Holy Spirit who guides us into **"all truth" (see John 16:13)** and teaches us **"all things" (see John 14:26)** than even the disciples who heard and knew Him in the flesh. Get this in your spirit. You can know Him more and walk in more revelation now, from the Holy Spirit's teaching, than the disciples who walked with Him. You can know Him better in the Spirit than the disciples knew Him in the flesh.

The disciples were looking for an earthly or political messiah. But after the Holy Spirit came on the day of Pentecost, they understood the true nature of the kingdom. Peter knew Jesus in the flesh and denied Him three times, but after he was filled with the Holy Spirit, he looked at persecution and said, **"Whether it is right in the sight of God to listen to you more than to God, you judge. For we cannot but speak the things which we have seen and heard" (Acts 4:19-20).** The apostles were bolder and more confident, powerful, and supernatural after Jesus left. They were willing to lay down their lives. So, what is hindering you?

We have it better with Christ with us and in us by the Spirit. This may be the most important truth you receive from this book. We are not led by our natural senses. After Jesus rose from the dead, He revealed a spiritual kingdom that delivers men from sin, not from emperors or dictators. The disciples understood this better after the resurrection.

Jesus told the disciples in John 16:13 that the Holy Spirit will speak only what He hears. The Holy Spirit teaches through dreams, visions, feelings, impressions, and words of knowledge. He speaks prophetically by revelation whatever He hears from the Father and Son. The Holy Spirit tells us what the Father and Son are saying if we will tune our ears to listen to Him. This is the one true God speaking in triune intimacy by the Spirit, not by the flesh. Instead of seeing Jesus in the flesh, we can receive impressions, feelings, dreams, and enter atmospheres. Words on a page or words of a song will jump out at us if we just tune our ears to listen.

The Father's and Son's thoughts are often about you! The Spirit listens and repeats what they are saying to us if we will listen with a trained ear and senses to the deliberations of the godhead. The Holy Spirit wants to tell you through an impression, dream, word of wisdom, or thought what the Father thinks about you. He will highlight specific things to you when you tune in to Him. You will hear the blueprint on the scroll of destiny for your life because you have taken to heart what this book can teach you and postured yourself to hear what is being said around the throne of God. His sheep hear His voice.

The Holy Spirit will share the Father's plans for each of us, even what our future holds. The Holy Spirit is like a "blabbermouth" who cannot wait to tell us everything the Father has for us. He does not judge us or withhold things from us. He wants to share everything with us if we are willing to listen. He does not ask us to be perfect before He shares anything with us.

We can know exactly where we need to be, what we need to say, and to whom we need to say it. The Spirit listens, and the Spirit speaks. He tells us of things to come. He doesn't try to keep us in the dark. We must break this stronghold in our thinking that God only speaks to the holy few, the pious, and the peculiar. No, the Holy Spirit presents Jesus to all of us through visions, dreams, impressions, words of knowledge, book titles, and even prophetic actions in movies. He will reveal Jesus to us. All of heaven's resources are ours.

It's so important that we have the Holy Spirit. We cannot physically see, hear, or touch the Holy Spirit, yet through Him, we can actually know Jesus better than the disciples did. Jesus told Thomas, **"Blessed are those who have not seen and yet have believed" (see John 20:29).** We are not second-class citizens of the kingdom because we did not know Him in the flesh. We get to spend our entire lives in the **"fellowship of the mystery" (see Ephesians 3:9).** **"For in Him we live and move and have our being" (see Acts 17:28).** Sometimes we start with just a sense or feeling, but then we start picking up the pieces of the puzzle until we see the full image. The spirit of prophecy and the testimony of Jesus always go together. The spirit of prophecy will tell us about Jesus because that's what the Holy Spirit does.

ALL WILL KNOW HIM

"But this is the covenant which I will make with the house of Israel after those days," declares the Lord, "I will put My law within them and on their heart I will write it; and I will be their God, and they shall be My people. They will not teach again, each man his neighbor and each man his brother, saying, 'Know the Lord,' for they will all know Me, from the least of them to the greatest of them," declares the Lord, "for I will forgive their iniquity, and their sin I will remember no more" (Jeremiah 31:33-34, NASB).

Here, Jeremiah prophesies about the covenant we are under today. We will *all* know Him. The Spirit, who is in your heart, enables you to know the Lord. He tears down every wall of division—age, gender, race, economic status, or social class—and transcends all distinctions. You will know the Lord no matter your earthly situation.

If we try to receive supernatural revelation by any means other than Christ, this is robbery and thievery, because access to the spirit realm is the inheritance of the children of the Lord. When God puts His law in our hearts, no one will need to be taught by his neighbor because all will know Him. There will come a time and place when no one will need to be led in how to know Him.

Under the fivefold ministry, we are growing in Him through words of knowledge, dreams, books, songs, nature, and more. Through prophetic revelation from the Holy Spirit, the Lord will communicate to us **"great and mighty things" (see Jeremiah 33:3)** which we do not know. Paul prayed to the Father in Ephesians 3 that God would strengthen us through His Spirit to know the width, length, depth, and height of God's love (see Ephesians 3:14-19). The Holy Spirit reveals all these things to us, without which we could never grasp or comprehend Him.

HOW TO HEAR THE VOICE OF GOD

The voice of God and the Spirit of God were synonymous to the Jewish people. The Spirit of God helps us know the voice of Jesus. God sent His voice to live inside us, so we could know and recognize Him. Jesus established this new covenant promise at the cross. This promise is based on the blood of Jesus, His passion, and His revealed love for us.

The indwelling Holy Spirit was put in us to hear the Good Shepherd. It is Jesus talking. The Spirit tells us what Jesus is saying through visions, impressions, words in a book, or words of a song we are hearing. Things jump off the page and speak to us. Imagery comes alive when we read Psalm 23. Such prophetic realities can convey more to us than any sermon ever could. This is a way to tune into the Spirit through your heart.

The Spirit of Truth is an active guide and counselor. Are you interested in the Holy Spirit, who can live in you to help you understand Jesus, know what He's speaking from day to day, receive direction from heaven about where and when to go, help you accurately interpret God's words, walk in the Spirit, and be a guide, helper, and counselor to others? Sign me up! This is what the prophetic is all about.

As teachers, we must take the complicated and break it down so it can be easily understood. This way, even an unlearned person can hear, understand, and know the voice of the Lord and know the prophetic in its simplest and most complicated forms.

How does the Holy Spirit speak? In every possible way we can imagine. Take every thought captive and discipline your mind (see 1 Corinthians 10:5) and you will hear. Watch your thoughts closely. You are not the sum total of your thoughts; you can live independent of your thoughts and control your thoughts by the power of the Holy Spirit. Don't let depressive thoughts fill your mind. Don't rehash past hurts in your mind. Stand guard and be the gatekeeper to your mind. Don't let your thoughts be controlled by whatever you see or hear.

Think about what you're thinking about. It may not be your thought. Perhaps you had a thought about something good or beautiful that is not something you would normally think about. Where did that thought come from? It may be the Holy Spirit trying to influence you. The voices of the spirit realm are like thoughts. Demons do not have vocal cords; neither does the Holy Spirit. You know what the Holy Spirit is saying because He speaks to you Spirit to spirit. However, if your spirit man is underdeveloped, you may not be able to hear the voice of the Spirit well. If you never give attention to the Word of God or to prayer, don't wonder why you never hear the Spirit's voice. We must develop our spirits because Spirit speaks to spirit.

DIFFERENT WAYS GOD SPEAKS

You may see someone you don't know and suddenly feel a deep sympathy and compassion for them or detect an illness in them or something else. If so, walk up to them and say, "Hello, ma'am. I don't know you, but I believe the Lord showed me something for you. You don't have to accept it, but could I share it?" If you hit the mark with them, you'll know you heard the voice of the Good Shepherd. It's easy to recognize your earthly father's voice after you have been listening to him for years. That is how you recognize the voice of the Holy Spirit—through repetition.

Thoughts come as words we hear or as mental pictures or strong visions. We need to determine if those mental pictures are from us or from the Holy Spirit. His sheep know His voice. You may even zone out for a while, which may be the Holy Spirit trying to communicate with you. Physically, you may be looking at a wall, yet not seeing the wall but something else instead.

Demons can also speak to us this way through fear, anxiety, depression, or discouragement. Angry thoughts can come to our mind about someone we're not even looking at or listening to. This can be a demonic voice. When we see things in our minds, this is called a vision. Visualize in your mind right now your favorite pet. What caused you to picture that pet? My suggestion.

What causes you to see other pictures in your mind? If you receive a thought or suggestion to pray for someone or some country that you know nothing about, that could be the Holy Spirit. Have you ever thought about or seen something in your mind, then physically saw it the next day? If so, the spirit world may be trying to communicate something to you. Have you ever thought to call someone, then the phone rang, and it was that person? That could be the Holy Spirit.

Have you ever had something happen to you in threes? This often speaks of a spiritual pattern. God may be trying to get you to forgive or to reconcile with someone. You can't stop thinking about them. Then someone else mentions them by name. Then you're watching television and the person in the show has the same name as the person with whom you need to reconcile. Or maybe you hear a song on the radio that you know is that person's favorite song. The Holy Spirit often works in threes.

God speaks to us through Scriptures, visions, pictures, dreams, and many other ways. I was driving home from a speaking engagement in Alabama when, in my mind, I saw my father-in-law driving. I saw the color of his suit, and I saw a car crash. I immediately called him and told him what I saw. He was driving to church. I described the road he was driving on. He confirmed that was where he was. I told him, "Don't go the normal way." So, he took a different route that ran parallel with the street he had been on. While on the other street, he saw ambulances and police cars rushing to the original street he had been on. This is just one way God speaks to us. Listen to the voice of the Shepherd. I could have said, "Well, that's a terrible thought to have. What if it turns out not to be true?" But I acted on it, and that is how we learn to know God's voice—by acting on it and putting it to the test.

The Lord also speaks through feelings, impressions, promptings, and intuition. One example of this is in Jesus's parable of the prodigal. Jesus said he sat in a pigpen and **"came to himself" (see Luke 15:17)**. He realized he could go back to his father's house. There was no audible voice that spoke or an angel that appeared to him; he just suddenly had an intuitive awakening to something he should have known all along. It was an impression, a moment. Impressions often come in the beginning stages of working in the prophetic. We feel something. A false or pseudo version of this is suspicion. Suspicion always has an accusatory element. Instead of believing the best in a person (see I Corinthians 13:7), we believe the worst.

God connects to us in many ways. He can speak through our own hearts and minds. We can even learn to hear His voice through other people. Sometimes a fitting word spoken at the right time is priceless. This is why we must always remain in fellowship and stay connected in small groups to maintain relationships.

God can also speak through nature or through the world around us. You may continually see a red cardinal appear, and through that, the Lord may give you a sense of Jesus' blood covering and cleansing you. That once happened to me. Psalm 23 describes the world around us: **"still waters;" "green pastures."** Mountains, valleys, and stars can communicate things to us. God can speak to us through virtually anything. You may go hiking on a walking trail and see something. I was on a walking trail and saw four numbers that represented the exact chapter and verse in the Bible I needed.

God can speak to us through pastoral invitations, Scripture readings, ministries, songs, movies, nature, art, road signs, numbers, license plates—you name it. If you want to be prophetic, be like Jesus who only did what He saw His Father do. He was like Forrest Gump; He showed up everywhere at just the right time, whether to turn water into wine or speak to a woman at a well. Look to God daily and let His word be a lamp to your feet and a light to your pathway (see Psalm 119:105).

HOW DO I KNOW IF IT'S GOD?

How do you know if what you hear is from the Lord? Filter it through Scripture. The voice of the Lord will never contradict His Word. There's a big difference between extrabiblical and unbiblical. God may tell you to go on a mission trip. That's not in the Bible; it's extrabiblical. However, taking a mission trip is never unbiblical. The Holy Spirit can help us discern what is from the Lord. We can also help weigh whether something is from the Lord by staying in community.

However, the best filters to discern whether something is the voice of the Spirit are the fruit of the Spirit and the Beatitudes. The voice of the Spirit is love, joy, peace, patience, kindness, goodness, faithfulness, gentleness, and self-control. These are relational communion words. When we listen to His voice, He will help us with relationships. He will say, "That's the voice of the flesh," or "that's the works of the flesh," or "this is the fruit of the Spirit."

The greatest sermon ever preached was Jesus' Sermon on the Mount. The voice of the Beatitudes is the same as the fruit of the Spirit. Is it poor in spirit? Does it have compassion for those who mourn? Is it meek or proud? Does it speak to hungering and thirsting for righteousness? Does it tell you to be merciful because you also need mercy? The voice of the flesh will speak carnality, retribution, vindication, and retaliation—this is the accuser of the brethren. Is there purity or pureness of heart in what was said? Does it lead you to be a peacemaker? The voice of the flesh is self-loathing, self-pity, grandiosity, boasting, exaggeration, pharisaism, violence, whining, and complaining.

DISCUSSION QUESTIONS

1. It's been said, "God speaks much less than many claim but much more than many hear." Do you agree with this statement? Why or why not?

2. In John 12:27-31, a voice spoke from heaven. Everyone heard something, yet there were three levels of hearing:

   (a) Some said, "It thundered,"
   (b) Others said, "An angel spoke,"
   (c) Jesus said, "This voice did not come because of Me, but for your sake" (the correct interpretation).

   Which level of hearing best describes your current level of hearing God's voice and why? Why do you think it's important that we all reach this third level?

3. How can we tell when we're experiencing something with a spiritual meaning or just experiencing something physical? What makes the difference? Explain.

4. Do you believe prophecy is a gift for all believers? Why or why not? Explain.

5. Jesus said in John 10:27, "My sheep hear My voice." How does this make you feel? In what ways do these words give you hope, comfort, or encouragement? Explain.

6. Why do you think the Spirit of God and the voice of God are often equated or the same in the Bible? Explain.

7. Describe a recent experience in which God may have spoken to you. What did He say? How did He speak to you? How did you know it was God? What happened as a result?

8. Name two ways in which you know God has spoken to you in the past (thoughts, mental pictures, visions, dreams, impressions, intuition, illuminations, senses, etc.). How does God normally or most commonly speak to you? Why do you think that is?

9. What are some of the ways we can know whether it was God who spoke to us?

PURPOSE FOR
the Prophetic

As another foundation stone, we must understand the purpose for the prophetic. As the children of Israel crossed over the Jordan, they picked up stones in the river to build an altar on the other side. For them, this meant they were "in it" for the long haul. We are also "in this" for the long haul and will try to cover all aspects of the prophetic in this book.

By definition, binocular fusion is the brain combining images from our two eyes to form a single visual perception. Essentially this means, though we have two eyes open, we visualize one uninterrupted scene. If we cover one eye, our vision is impaired, and the range of what we see is limited. However, when both eyes are combined, we still see a single image through two individual scenes or two separate eyes.

PROPHETIC BINOCULAR FUSION

Moses experienced prophetic binocular fusion. He wrote the first five books of the Bible. He lived hundreds of years after creation, yet he could write about it as if he was there. After he came down from Mount Sinai, he had to put a veil over his face, because his face shined so brightly with the glory of God the people could not look at him. When he was in the spirit realm, he could see in the past (the creation in Genesis 1-3), and before he

29

died, he could also see in the future (the land of promise) though he could not enter it (see Deuteronomy 34:4).

How can a man who lived in the human time realm write about events that existed before his birth and also see into the future? Because his eyes were opened to see with prophetic binocular fusion. Just as a brain can use images from two eyes to create one big picture, the Holy Spirit can help us see the spiritual big picture. The spirit realm is not bound by the present. It sees all eternity. Eternity is the domain of God, **"Who was and is and is to come!" (see Revelation 4:8).**

Every day we can see through our natural eyes. We drive to work, we see people, we recognize co-workers and family members, and we see trees and nature and recognize natural beauty. Being prophetic is when we can live our lives and be relevant in the earthly time realm while simultaneously seeing by grace, faith, and the Spirit what God allows us to see in the eternal spirit realm, that is unbound by time. Because of the Spirit, we can see the past and future realms now. In the spirit realm, the past and future are now, yet outside time.

SEEING THE PAST AND THE FUTURE

When the prophets of old, like Isaiah, prophesied the birth of Jesus seven hundred years before Christ's birth, they were seeing things in the spirit realm where everything was already finished, though it had not yet happened in the earthly time realm. Isaiah wrote, **"For unto us <u>a Child is born</u>, unto us <u>a Son is given</u>: and the government will be upon His shoulder. And His name will be called Wonderful, Counselor, Mighty God, Everlasting Father, Prince of Peace" (Isaiah 9:6).** He spoke as if it had already happened.

He also prophesied in Isaiah 53 about the "Man" who would be marred beyond recognition, wounded for our transgressions, and bruised for our iniquities (see Isaiah 53:2-5). Isaiah wasn't guessing; he was seeing. The Spirit of the Lord came to Isaiah seven hundred years before these earthly events happened. While Isaiah worked in his daily life, the Lord allowed him, by the Spirit, to peer into the spirit realm, peel back the veil, and see shutter glimpses into the future. This included shutter glimpses of the virgin-born Son of God and of His stripes and wounds for our healing.

So, before we can partner with eternity and all there is to see and behold, and bring it to the present, we must understand that eternity is not bound by time. Everything that will eventually happen in time has already happened in the spirit realm. Jesus peeled back the veil, so we could see shutter glimpses of both His past and His future.

> **For we who have believed do enter that rest, as He has said: "So I swore in My wrath, 'They shall not enter My rest,'" although the works were finished from the foundation of the world (Hebrews 4:3).**

> **All who dwell on the earth will worship him, whose names have not been written in the Book of Life of the Lamb slain from the foundation of the world (Revelation 13:8).**

Jesus, the Lamb, was slain from the foundation of the world. Jesus was born about four thousand years after Adam in the earthly time realm. However, in the Spirit and mind of God, the Logos, the plan, the idea, the Word that was with God, was already made flesh and dwelt among us (see John 1:1-3, 14). Galatians 4:4 says, **"But when the fullness of the time had come, God sent forth His Son, born of a woman, born under the law."** This means, in the Spirit, there is a fullness of time for things to be manifested.

Another example is when Jesus prayed in the garden and asked the Father to give Him the glory He had with Him before the world was (see John 17:5). Jesus did not experience this as a physical man, but rather in the spirit realm, as the Son of God. Jesus asked God to reveal in the earthly time realm, the glory He and the Father shared from before the creation of the world because, according to the blueprint of heaven, the fullness of time *had* come. The glory He had shared with the Father in eternity would now be accomplished at the cross, where the finished work was to be manifested in the earthly time realm, though He was **"slain from the foundation of the world."** He had to live a sinless life, die, be buried, and ascend back to heaven in the earthly time realm for us to now preach the finished work of Christ.

In Genesis 17:5, God said to Abram, **"I have made you a father of many nations."** How could God call him a **"father of many nations"** before he even had a child? God called Abram to be a father long before Ishmael and Isaac were born. God can do that because He predestined us according to His foreknowledge, though we still have free will. In fact, many of the events in our lives were ordained long before we were born.

God told Jeremiah, **"Before I formed you in the womb, I knew you; before you were born I sanctified you; I ordained you a prophet to the nations" (Jeremiah 1:5).** Before Jeremiah became even a twinkle in his father's eye, based on foreknowledge, God predestined events in Jeremiah's life which were preplanned in the spirit realm.

In all things, we must cooperate with the Word and the Spirit, because the Word and the Spirit agree. Our depth in the Word will coincide with our depth in the Spirit. Romans 4:17 says, **"(As it is written, 'I have made you a father of many nations') in the presence of Him whom he believed—God, who gives life to the dead and calls those things which do not exist as**

though they did." This is profound. God declares things in the Spirit before time even enters the equation, as though they had already happened in the earthly time realm.

THREE STEPS OF THE PROPHETIC

Now if you aspire to be a prophetic person, don't get hung up on titles. Just say, "I aspire to be a prophetic voice." That is not presumptuous. There is a difference between the gift of prophecy and the office of a prophet. Paul said all believers may prophesy, but not all are prophets (see 1 Corinthians 12:29, 14:31). I have seen prophetic people who adamantly wanted to be called prophets. I was a pastor for twelve years, but I didn't feel a need to be called a "pastor," because I *did* the work of a pastor.

God calls prophets and prophetic voices to see the finished works of God in the spirit realm. Then, as God's mouthpieces, prophets speak what they see in the Spirit. They speak through words the images they see in the Spirit. They see what the Father sees in the Spirit. The first step to encountering the spirit realm is to see what the Father sees; then speak whatever images we see. Then finally, it manifests. So, the three steps to the prophetic are: 1) see it, 2) speak it, 3) watch it manifest.

These manifestations come through words, and these words are the expressions of the Logos—the thought, plan, and idea of God contained in the Spirit. This is not "name it, claim it;" this is about what God shows us in the Spirit. Then we speak, and those words bring what was finished in the eternal realm into manifestation in the earthly time realm. In other words, the fullness of time comes.

We are all taught to pray the Lord's Prayer: **"Your will** [plan, purpose] **be done on earth as it** [already] **is in heaven" (see**

Matthew 6:10). God's will has already been finished in heaven. We bring things from the finished heavenly realm to the earthly time realm, so God's plans can be manifested on earth. How can we know the Father is showing something to us? This comes with practice. God can work through our senses that are consecrated to the Lord (see Hebrews 5:14). There is a prophetic blueprint of history in the spirit realm. We are called to declare through words, what we have seen in the Spirit, so it will be manifested.

Jesus made a strong statement in John 5:19: **"Most assuredly, I say to you, the Son can do nothing of Himself, but what He sees the Father do; for whatever He does, the Son also does in like manner."** The reason this can happen to the sons of God is because of verse 20: **"For the Father loves the Son, and shows Him all things that He Himself does; and He will show Him greater works than these, that you may marvel."** The Father did it in heaven before the Son did it on earth. The Father has already done it. We are just waiting for the fullness of time to manifest here in the earthly time realm what has already manifested in the heavenly realm. To this day, I have never gotten over just how incredible this is. Every time a revelation comes true, no matter how great or small, it's incredible how this works.

You may ask, "But what if I'm *not* a prophet? What if I'm just what Paul said, 'For you can all prophesy one by one'?" Well, are you a son or daughter of God? He shows the Son all things, not just the prophets. Are we not also sons and daughters of the Father? This is our inheritance—to see in the Spirit, speak as oracles or mouthpieces of God, and bring things to pass on earth. We see it, speak it, and it manifests until God's kingdom is fully manifest on earth. I believe we will see much more of the kingdom here on earth before Jesus returns. I don't know how much we'll see this side of the second coming, but I am believing for the whole kit and caboodle.

"Whatever we can see here, Lord, may we be the conduit and mouthpiece to speak Your Logos through our lips and bring it to realization." What if more than just a few prophets on earth could see it, speak it, and see it manifested? What if an entire *company* of prophets could see it, speak it, and see it manifested? We could bring more pieces of the kingdom into manifestation and have more manifestations of His glory before the second coming.

SEE IT

Amos 3:7 says, **"Surely the Lord God does nothing, unless He reveals His secret to His servants the prophets."** That is why we are here, to bring the kingdom—one impression at a time, one dream at a time, one vision at a time, one trance at a time—and speak it into reality. Hunger to see into the treasure chest of heaven. We don't need to acquiesce as the world gets darker. Here is what I know: The light will become brighter daily for those who walk in the path of life, the path of the righteous.

The seeing or "seer" realm is not reserved for the few but for all sons and daughters of God. Fill your mind and subconscious mind with the Word of God, for this will have a major effect on your soul. If you're the type of person whose dreams are based on fears like falling or based on your daily experiences, then your subconscious mind is flowing from your soul. The more you fill your mind with the Word, the more you will create an atmosphere in which God can work through your subconscious mind to speak, teach, and train your soul.

Seeing in the Spirit and then seeing that manifest in the natural is prophetic binocular fusion. The purpose of the prophetic is to reveal the Father's heart, plans, and good pleasure. The Spirit of God in the future fuses with our spirits in the present. We speak of what we see fused with the future Spirit of

God, and we can speak that future into the present. Psychics speak *about* the future; prophets *create* the future. Psychics pervert the holy. Again, Amos 3:7 says, **"Surely the Lord God does nothing, unless He reveals His secret to His servants the prophets."** Have you ever felt there should be more of God in your life, church, ministry, or family? Well, the Lord does nothing until He reveals it to His servants the prophets.

Aside from what the written Word of God tells us will happen, which is forever settled in heaven, we can determine what will happen in everyday life by cooperating with the Holy Spirit. He waits to do something until we see it, speak it, and it manifests. If you want more of God in your life, family, and church, hunger to see into heaven's treasure chest. The Lord wants to share His secrets with His friends (see John 15:15). Actions in the physical realm are framed by prophets who see **"on earth as it is in heaven."** God wants to see prophetic participation and cooperation in our lives, families, and cultures.

SPEAK IT

How much of the heavenly blueprint remains unfulfilled on earth because prophetic voices are not speaking what they see in the secret place? How many missed opportunities have there been because prophets and prophetic voices are not speaking into existence what they see? The written Word of God has already declared the overall plan of God. This is **"Forever ... settled in heaven" (see Psalm 119:89)**, but how many of the microcosmic plans of God in our lives are missed because we do not speak them? God is waiting for our participation. How many believers have missed the time of their visitation because they weren't expecting God to show them His blueprint through visions, dreams, visitations, or impressions? God waits to do some things until they are spoken. Words have the power to create and rearrange the future. We can come to agreement with His highest plans and purposes for our lives to co-create our future.

As prophetic people, we can walk in a realm where we affect the future by speaking what we see in the heavenly blueprint of God's good plans from His heavenly scrolls. We can impact our lives, purposes, callings, cultures, and governments by speaking into existence what is in the Spirit. What did the Lamb of God say? **"I have come that they may have life, and that they may have it more abundantly" (see John 10:10).** The Bible contains the full expression of the life we can live in God, the God kind of life, but are we even seeing that? One of the biggest purposes of this book is to help raise up a company of seers, speakers, and manifesters. You are reading this because you are serious about doing this.

Mark 11:23 says, **"For assuredly, I say to you, whoever says to this mountain, 'Be removed and be cast into the sea,' and does not doubt in his heart, but believes that those things he says will be done, he will have whatever he says."** We cannot speak and move mountains until we first see from heaven's blueprint that a mountain stands in our way.

FREQUENCY VIBRATIONS

Genesis 1:1 says, **"In the beginning God created..."** *Created* is the Hebrew word *bara*. The Hebrew alphabet contains twenty-two letters. Each letter has a light and frequency vibration associated with it. When David played his harp in the field as a shepherd, his harp also had twenty-two strings. I believe that, as David played his harp, he sent out frequency vibrations that helped frame his future as king. These vibrations resonated with Samuel when Samuel went to Jesse's home to anoint the king. None of David's brothers seemed right to Samuel. That's why

Samuel asked Jesse, **"Are all the young men here?"** Jesse said, **"There remains yet the youngest keeping the sheep."** Samuel said, **"Send and bring him" (see 1 Samuel 16:11-12).** There was resonance and agreement when Samuel met David.

In our meetings, the "frequency" of our meetings should match the "frequency" of heaven. When heaven plucks an "e" string on a guitar, we want that to resonate here on earth where we also pluck the "e" string. We want God's glory in our midst to be real. We want His Spirit to take over our meetings. We want people healed. We want people to receive ministry. Whatever frequency heaven emits, we want to make sure we're vibrating on that same frequency.

Very often the culture we embrace matches the music to which we listen. If we listen to beer-drinking, cheating-on-our-spouses songs, our lives will greatly reflect this. Our personal state of mind will often match the frequency emanating from the songs to which we listen.

Create in Hebrew means to form or shape. The first letter of the word "create" is *bet*, which means a vessel or container. The second is the Hebrew letter *dalet*, which means a gate or door. The third letter is *aleph*, which means to create something out of nothing. So, in Genesis 1:1, God had a blueprint from heaven for all of creation. **"In the beginning God created"** means He spoke a vessel, brought it through a gate or door, and created something out of nothing. When God created in Genesis 1, He used a container called "words" (which is a vibration or frequency), and it opened up the door (which is Christ) to release the *aleph* (which is illuminated light). The *aleph* is made up of two *yods*, which represent the higher and lower or seen and unseen realms. There is even a *vav* between the two *yods*, which connects the two realms together. This is binocular fusion.

38

The three letters of the Hebrew word *bara* (create) actually show us how the spirit world translates what is finished in the spirit realm into the fullness of the earthly time realm. God uses words, through Christ, to create something out of nothing. Likewise, when we prophesy, we are using words through the door (Christ) to create something out of nothing. That is why, when we prophesy, our words do not fall to the ground. The occult world, like a thief and a robber, tries to do this through a back door, and their words *do* fall to the ground because they do not operate through Christ.

So, practically speaking, what does all this look like? God may show me a woman in a crowd. I may see a vision that someone has cancer. I might also see that this woman is wearing a purple shirt. I see all this in the Spirit and speak what I see. Maybe I saw in a vision that she is cancer-free. I saw the blueprint of heaven; I spoke the blueprint of heaven through words or through the Logos Word (Christ), then it manifested. Prophecy brings things from the eternal spirit realm to this earthly time realm.

THE SCREEN OF OUR MINDS

Our souls can be subject to our spirits or our flesh. This determines the kind of life we will live. We are tripart beings— spirit, soul, and body. The Lord wants to have most of our beings —spirit and soul. We must bring our souls into subjection to our spirits, so our spirits can become our dominating part, and so our spirits can be released through us to others.

For the weapons of our warfare are not carnal, but mighty through God to the pulling down of strong holds; casting down <u>imaginations</u>, and every high thing that exalteth itself against the knowledge of God, and bringing into captivity every <u>thought</u> to the obedience of Christ; and having in a

readiness to revenge all disobedience, when your obedience is fulfilled (2 Corinthians 10:4-6 KJV).

There are two words we need to pay attention to here in verse 5—thoughts and imaginations. Every thought must become captive to the obedience of Christ. If we have sanctified imaginations, God can tell us more. Our eyes are the light of our souls (see Matthew 6:22). This means, don't watch, or look at ungodly things. We must keep our thoughts in subjection and say, "My mind belongs to the Lord." Don't let "R-rated" mental movies play on the screen of your mind.

There are three possible imagination projectors in our minds: Satan's, ours, and the Holy Spirit's. We have one screen, but three projectors are vying for the right to project onto our screens. Satan can control the eyes of our minds when we don't sanctify our eyes and our imaginations. Job said, **"I have made a covenant with my eyes; why then should I look upon a young woman?" (Job 31:1)** Pornography can greatly hinder the spiritual screens of our minds.

Our imaginations often have a "replay button" for past traumas, shame, and guilt. To take captive every thought, we must think about what we're thinking about and choose what we think about. We must stop the repetitive mental movies that can lead to depression, suicide, unforgiveness, or bitterness. It all starts with playing unsanctified mental movies. We may curse our imaginations as instruments of the devil, not realizing those imaginations can be sanctified. We can also fulfill the prophecies of what Satan projects in our minds. Jesus said He could only do what He saw His Father doing (see John 5:19). That means He saw it on the screen of His mind. That is how we act on prophetic words.

Satan will supply us with endless sources of pictures if we let him. These pictures will create feelings of doubt, worry, or lack of self-worth. "Oh, it will be bad. It will be awful. I can just see this turning into a big fight. What if this or that happens?" These are all bad visions. Whatever we see play over and over in our minds, we begin to believe, then live it. Our imaginations have huge potential—both good and bad. Our ability to see and imagine things in the Spirit is an incredible gift. We must rise and reclaim this gift for God's purposes.

In the Old Testament, adultery was an act, but Jesus said, **"whoever *looks* at a woman to lust for her has already committed adultery with her in his heart" (see Matthew 5:28,** emphasis added). We must shut off the movie. I can choose the attitude by which I look at a woman. I just see them as someone's daughter. We can create a reality or a fantasy in our minds. We can also prime the pump for the Lord by setting the scenes that Jesus wants to use to communicate with us. It is the Father's good pleasure to do this.

> **I saw in the visions of my head while on my bed, and there was a watcher, a holy one, coming down from heaven. He cried aloud and said thus:**
>
> **"Chop down the tree and cut off its branches, strip off its leaves and scatter its fruit. Let the beasts get out from under it, and the birds from its branches. Nevertheless leave the stump and roots in the earth" (see Daniel 4:13-15).**

While we are praying, we may see someone in our minds. We may see something the Lord wants to do in their lives. Or, we may see something the Lord is saying about our own lives. These are actually encounters with God. King Nebuchadnezzar encountered an angel in a vision in his mind. We need to know which projector is playing in our minds. We need to know the difference between our thoughts/projector and God's thoughts/projector. This is the difference between prophecy and "vain imaginations" (see Romans 1:21 KJV).

In the first year of Belshazzar king of Babylon, Daniel had a dream and <u>visions of his head while on his bed</u>. Then he wrote down the dream, telling the main facts.

Daniel spoke, saying, "<u>I saw in my vision by night</u>, and behold, the four winds of heaven were stirring up the Great Sea"

<u>I was watching in the night visions</u>, and behold, One like the Son of Man, coming with the clouds of heaven!

I, Daniel, was grieved in my spirit within my body, and <u>the visions of my head troubled me</u> (see Daniel 7:1-2, 13, 15).

These were all mental visions in the night, the projector of the Holy Spirit projecting on the screen of Daniel's mind. The more we read the Word of God and meditate on it, the more we can play movies in our minds while reading the Word. For example, picture Psalm 23 as you read it: **"He makes me to lie down in green pastures; He leads me beside the still waters."** Scripture reading can be a doorway to a mental vision.

The Word of God begins to assimilate and become a part of us. The assimilated word of God is living, powerful, and sharper than any two-edged sword, dividing between the soul and spirit and joints and marrow (see Hebrews 4:12). "Joints and marrow" mean the word can discern diseases. The word of God can do through us physically what it does through us spiritually. We can know and discern diseases. We can also know and discern the thoughts and intents of our hearts. Get God's Word in you!

SEEING AND HEARING

Our capacities to see and hear on a spiritual level are the two main ways the Lord speaks to us.

And I will make your descendants as the dust of the earth; so that if a man could number the dust of the earth, then your descendants also could be numbered. Arise, walk in the land through its length and its width, for I give it to you.

Then Abram moved his tent, and went and dwelt by the terebinth trees of Mamre, which are in Hebron, and built an altar there to the Lord (Genesis 13:16-18).

Then He brought him outside and said, "<u>Look now toward heaven, and count the stars if you are able to number them</u>." And He said to him, "So shall your descendants be."

And he believed in the Lord, and He accounted it to him for righteousness (Genesis 15:5-6).

The Lord gave Abraham a picture of his *rhema* word, telling him to look up in the sky. This produced faith in him and made it possible for Abraham to be steady until it actually happened. This belief moved what he saw from his head to his heart. Romans 10:10 says, **"For with the heart one believes unto righteousness, and with the mouth confession is made unto salvation."** The mouth confesses what the heart believes. Seeing with our spiritual eyes is seeing with the projector of our imaginations. Balaam the prophet was highly respected as an accurate prophet.

And Balaam raised his eyes, and saw Israel encamped according to their tribes; and the Spirit of God came upon him.

Then he took up his oracle and said:

"The utterance of Balaam the son of Beor, the utterance of the man whose eyes are opened, the utterance of him who hears the words of God, who sees the vision of the Almighty, who falls down, with eyes wide open (Numbers 24:2-4).

So he took up his oracle and said:

"The utterance of Balaam the son of Beor, and the utterance of the man whose eyes are opened; the utterance of him who hears the words of God, and has the knowledge of the Most High, who sees the vision of the Almighty, who falls down, with eyes wide open (Numbers 24:15-16).

The prophetic is all about seeing and hearing with our spiritual eyes and ears. Jesus saw things in a visionary sense.

Then Jesus answered and said to them, "Most assuredly, I say to you, the Son can do nothing of Himself, but what He sees the Father do; for whatever He does, the Son also does in like manner. For the Father loves the Son, and shows Him all things that He Himself does" (see John 5:19-20).

The Father wants to communicate through us, through the Holy Spirit projector, to show us what the Father is doing. Later, Jesus said He spoke the things He spoke with the Father. **"All these things Jesus spoke to the multitude in parables; and without a parable He did not speak to them" (Matthew 13:34).** Jesus spoke in parables, so they could see present spiritual realities. For example, Jesus saw vines heavy with fruit as an image of our fruitfulness when abiding in Him. **"He is the image of the invisible God, the firstborn over all creation" (Colossians 1:15).** Jesus Himself is also the image of the invisible God.

DISCUSSION QUESTIONS

1. In your own words, explain binocular fusion.

2. In your own words, explain prophetic binocular fusion.

3. Give a scriptural example of someone seeing in the past.

4. Give a scriptural example of someone seeing the future.

5. Explain the *process* of prophetic binocular fusion. How exactly does this work? (It has something to do with the eternal spirit realm and the earthly time realm.)

6. Name the three steps of the prophetic.

7. Why are prophets also known as "seers"?

8. Why is speaking what we see so important to the prophetic?

9. What do "frequency vibrations" have to do with the prophetic?

10. What are the "three imagination projectors" that can play in our minds?

11. How can we control which imagination projector plays in our minds? Explain.

12. What are the two main ways the Lord speaks to us?

13. Which of the two ways does the Lord speak mostly to you? Why do you think that is?

"Things can be revealed in dreams that surpass
what we know in the natural world."

PARTS OF
the Prophetic

When we understand that **"God is Spirit" (see John 4:24)**, we will understand that God speaks spiritual languages. Just as humans speak human languages using human vocal sounds, vibrations, and dialects, God speaks a spiritual language. Since God *is* Spirit, He does not have vocal cords like we do. This means, most of the time, His voice will not be audible as our voices are when we communicate. This does *not* mean God cannot speak audibly; it simply means, most of the time, God speaks Spirit to spirit, not Spirit to flesh.

This also means our spirits must be developed to a degree that we can understand His spiritual language. God often speaks through pictures, images, impressions, dreams, visions, and trances. Visions and trances are like having dreams while you're awake. One reason God often speaks to us through dreams is because our conscious minds are more relaxed while we sleep, and much of the brain chatter that continues during our daily activities temporarily shuts down.

> **For God may speak in one way, or in another, yet man does not perceive it. In a dream, in a vision of the night, when deep sleep falls upon men, while slumbering on their beds, then He opens the ears of men, and seals their instruction. In order to turn man from his deed, and conceal pride from man, He keeps back his soul from the**

Pit, and his life from perishing by the sword (Job 33:14-18).

What an incredible description of how God speaks. Notice God is not limited to speaking in just one way; He speaks **"in one way, or in another."** By learning to identify the various ways God speaks, we can learn to process the prophetic and not limit God to one form of communication. Job 33 confirms that, when we sleep, our brain chatter stops long enough for God to bypass our conscious minds and speak to our subconscious minds. He can then use mental pictures or movies to speak to us through visions and dreams.

Job 33:16 says, **"He opens the ears of men."** The most important step in processing the prophetic is God opening our ears to hear His instructions. This verse clearly implies that a person's spiritual ears can be shut. So, first we need God to open our ears, so we can learn His language. This begins the prophetic process of hearing, interpretation, and application.

Job 33 also explains the benefits of hearing from God. Hearing can keep us from sinning, help us make a U-turn when we're heading in the wrong direction, or prevent us from destruction, or even losing our lives. This is why processing the prophetic is so important, and why it's absolutely imperative that we learn how God speaks.

DREAMS

God can speak through dreams, but we need to recognize when a dream is from God or when it's a "pizza dream" from the pizza we ate the night before. Have you ever had a dream that stuck out to you so much you couldn't forget it? Maybe you knew it had special meaning, but you didn't know what that special meaning was.

The Old Testament gives us the template for New Testament prophetic giftings through visions and dreams, which accompany Holy Spirit activity. **"And it shall come to pass afterward, that I will pour out My Spirit upon all flesh; your sons and your daughters shall prophesy, your old men shall dream dreams, your young men shall see visions" (Joel 2:28).**

Peter quoted this verse on the day of Pentecost. Young men are more inclined to have visions of the future because they're young, but old people can also have visions, and young people can also have dreams.

Dreams play an important role in the lives of prophetic people. They can serve as keys to understanding the real you. Things can be exposed in dreams that surpass what we know in the natural world. Dreams can speak to our potential or reveal things already lurking within us. They can speak to our fears. God can even use our dreams to minister deliverance to us.

For the unconsecrated mind (a mind that's not being regularly filled with the Word of God but with other things), dreams often reveal what is lurking inside. They usually come in the form of pictures, emotions, or feelings that our subconscious minds project. However, sometimes God will superimpose a dream on an unconsecrated mind to reveal His purpose, a necessary truth, a warning, or a reality that could either save their life or reveal His will for their life. Most people just feel like they dream about their worst fears.

Our spirit man never sleeps, and since "God is Spirit," He never sleeps either. Some people have trouble shutting down their minds at night, but the spirit of our minds can be renewed (see Ephesians 4:23). The spiritual function of our brains can go far beyond what our minds, wills, and emotions can do. Our inner man is always awake, so God can teach us things even while we sleep. Joseph learned to take Jesus and Mary to Egypt and hide them from Herod while he slept.

Young's Bible Dictionary defines a vision as "a means by which God transfers information to people which otherwise would not be available to them." It defines a dream as "a vision received while asleep." A vision is simply a dream you have when you're awake; a dream is a vision you have when you're asleep. *Webster's Dictionary* defines a dream as "an image or idea present in the sleeping mind" and a vision as "the act or capability of seeing."

The Hebrew word for "dream" is *halom*. It can mean ordinary dreams during sleep, but it can also mean prophetic dreams or visionary experiences, which are different from impressions. You may have an impression in your spirit. "I felt impressed to..." is a common expression among prophetic people. Prophetic people often receive communications from God through visions and dreams. If you believe the only way to hear from God is through tongues and interpretation, then that is the only way you will hear from God. The Pentecostal movement built a doctrine and campfire around tongues and interpretation, yet there is much more to the prophetic than this.

Personally, I have prophesied, spoken in tongues, and spoken the truths of God in my dreams, but this started happening after I intentionally desired to center my entire being on the Lord. "Help us, Lord, to learn the difference between our thoughts and dreams and Your thoughts and dreams and give us the grace to interpret those dreams."

INTERPRETATION OF DREAMS

Dreams are a series of thoughts, emotions, and feelings that occur while sleeping. A small percentage of dreams foretell future events, but more times than not, dreams contain symbols we must accurately interpret. We must figure out the symbolism 95% of the time. I know of a woman who dreamed her son was drowning in a lake. She went outside, saw he had fallen through the ice, and was able to save him from drowning. Only 5% of our dreams are based on literal events like this one; the rest are symbolic.

Here are some examples of universal dream language interpretation. It is said that individuals who often appear in our dreams represent a part of ourselves seeking repression or expression. Perhaps you're making a courageous decision about taking your kids out of public schools and teaching them at home, though you know it will be a real challenge. So, who might show up in your dreams? The most bold and courageous person you've ever met.

Or you could have a dream that your pastor did something immoral or underhanded. But remember, less than 5% of our dreams are based on literal events. So, God may be showing you the *shadow* of a person to whom you can relate. God may even be exposing a part of *you* that needs to be brought under control. How often do we see things in others we don't want to address in ourselves? A critical spirit is often just a picture of ourselves that is easier to address in others. God may be trying to address a part of your character in love.

If you watch soap operas all day, you'll dream about soap operas. If you think about business all day, you'll dream about business. Dreams have an inherent language. They're usually a type, shadow, or reflection of reality. Learning so-called "universal" dream symbols can be helpful, but they're not always "universal." Some dream language interpretations have universal meanings, others do not, and at best, maybe 30% of universal symbols have relevance. A symbol to you may mean something totally different than what it means to me. We cannot use symbols to create cookie-cutter dreams.

Have you ever dreamed something that didn't make sense? Discover the potential message *behind* what doesn't make sense. Delivery drivers may dream about packages because that's what they see all day. Dreams can bring direction, but more often they bring confirmation. There's nothing wrong with asking for a second opinion about a dream. However, that person may not know the symbols God uses for your own experiences or for your own frame of reference or prophetic filter.

What if you have a dream that you're pregnant? I've had ladies tell me, "I dreamed I was pregnant." One said, "I saw a baby boy in my dream." I asked, "What does the concept of a baby boy mean to you?" She said, "It makes me think of something new being born." As it turned out, God was trying to tell her that something new was being birthed in her life, not that she would have a literal baby. We need to understand the meaning of symbols. There are exceptions, but more times than not, God uses dreams to warn or reveal something about our lives.

On October 9, 2023, during our nine-month MorningStar School of the Prophets, which consists of one Thursday-Saturday weekend a month, we were involved in intense teachings, activations, and trainings, when I called out a female student whose last name was "Luther." I said I saw a spirit of reformation on her. Instantly, I saw the Holy Spirit come over her and physically affect her. Then I saw a vision of Martin Luther famously nailing his Ninety-five Theses to the door of Wittenberg's Castle Church, officially beginning the Protestant Reformation.

I said, "I see this as a dream that was experienced, and I see this playing out as a mental movie right now before my eyes." This dear lady replied in front of the crowd, "I did have a dream about Martin Luther nailing the scroll on the door of Wittenberg Church with a large hammer and nails, and heard Martin Luther say to me, 'This is why your name is "Luther."'" She confirmed she had this dream but only shared it privately with her husband. That night, a secret of her heart was revealed through a word of knowledge.

JOSEPH'S DREAM

The Old Testament story of Joseph contains a wealth of knowledge about prophetic dreams.

> **"Now Joseph had a dream, and he told it to his brothers; and they hated him even more. So he said to them, 'Please hear this dream which I have dreamed: There we were, binding sheaves in the field. Then behold, my sheaf arose and also stood upright; and indeed your sheaves stood all around and bowed down to my sheaf'" (Genesis 37:5-7).**

Have you ever seen a sheaf or bundle of wheat bowing in a dream? These symbols and actions of these symbols appeared real to Joseph, though they defied logic. God will speak to us using symbols we can relate to, and that's why "universal" dream symbols are not always "universal." Since Joseph spent time in the field, God spoke to him through a symbol to which he could relate. If Joseph were an auto mechanic, perhaps he would have seen cars standing up and bowing to other cars. God uses whatever field with which we are familiar because God uses the familiar to bring understanding to the unfamiliar.

God will use our culture, imagery, and language to ensure we grasp what He is trying to convey to us in a vision or dream. In reality, Joseph wasn't seeing sheaves bowing down to one another, those sheaves represented him and his brothers. Joseph was seeing God elevating him over his brothers. Understanding our dream language and symbolisms is key to developing our prophetic filters.

Thankfully, Joseph did not misinterpret his dream. Had he, he might have thought he was a literal sheaf or might turn into one. That is why I believe that others cannot fully interpret our dreams. They can certainly help, but ultimately, we must interpret our own dreams because God speaks *our* language.

For example, we cannot fully appreciate something from the Greek language if we don't speak Greek. Many people experience dreams that are evil or sinful in nature. This could indicate they are giving their minds over to movies that act out such things, so they dream such things. This could also indicate an area where God wants to expose a thief or robber present in their body, which is His temple (see 1 Corinthians 6:19).

There were many dreamers in Scripture—Jacob, Joseph, Job, and Joseph (Mary's husband). Jacob saw a ladder with angels ascending and descending. When he woke up from that dream, he said, **"Surely the Lord is in this place, and I did not know it" (see Genesis 28:16).** The patriarch, Joseph, had great dreams. Both Joseph and Daniel were known for interpreting others' dreams. We must learn to interpret God's voice accurately.

Dreams have messages. Joseph's dream had a message, and his brothers hated him for it. It sounded like a "pizza dream" that didn't make sense. Sheaves of wheat bowing to another sheaf of wheat makes no sense in the natural, but God speaks languages and uses symbols we can relate to from past experiences. This is called our prophetic filter. Joseph could relate to wheat like delivery drivers can relate to packages.

For Joseph, the sheaves of wheat represented him and his brothers. It wasn't a literal dream, but it represented something literal. Joseph should have known who and who not to share the dream with and the right time to share it. Our dreams can hurt us when we don't share them with the right people or at the right time. Sometimes, others will react negatively to our dreams.

Joseph knew the interpretation. He shared it, and this delayed the promise of God in his life by twenty years. His brothers' reaction was not good. This is another reason we should not leave the interpretation of our dreams to others. Others can help, but we should always ask God to give us the interpretation and advise about when or even *if* we should share our dreams. Personally, I have learned *not* to share my dreams with all Christians, as some will call it "the devil" or "the occult" because they don't understand the prophetic.

I have sometimes misinterpreted things that I have prophesied to others. I once prophesied to a person about being generous. I saw a McDonald's sign and misinterpreted that to mean the restaurant chain when I should have related it to the Ronald McDonald Charities. My word to them was about how the Lord would use them to bless people, but at the time I didn't make the connection or accurately interpret what I saw. Just because we don't agree with something a prophetic person says, that doesn't make them our enemy. God is calling us to raise *up* an end-time army, not shoot each other *down*.

I was furious when so many prophets "threw in the towel" because people got mad at them when their prophecies about President Donald Trump being re-elected didn't come to pass. Our prophets were shot down by friendly fire. Pray for the prophets. The Bible defines false prophets as those who lead God's people to worship false gods (see Jeremiah 7:8-11, 23:13, 27), not those whose prophecies are delayed or nefariously altered by human will. Let's agree on that.

In Daniel 2, Daniel prophesied to a government leader. The prophetic can bring us great influence with government leaders, business leaders, and many others (see Proverbs 18:16). King Nebuchadnezzar had a dream that others could not interpret. He even threatened the lives of all his prophets and astrologers for not being able to interpret his dream. He wanted them to tell him the contents and interpretation of his dream. Daniel, the prophet of God, prayed and received revelation and the interpretation of Nebuchadnezzar's dream. This greatly elevated Daniel in the empire and made governmental leaders trust the prophetic and recognize **"there is a God in heaven who reveals secrets"** (see **Daniel 2:28**).

The Holy Spirit communicates to us through visions and dreams as part of His revelations. It is paramount that we understand the symbolism and everything else that goes along with visions and dreams. We must understand what they are, who they're for, why they come, and then believe God for more visions and dreams.

Recurring dreams could indicate a very important message or truth that we are not grasping. Some dreams can stop, then pick up right where we left off the next time we sleep. Finally, in seeking the interpretation of dreams, whenever we discover the true interpretation, it will immediately resonate with us.

Remember, we are tripart beings—spirit, soul, and body—so our cycle of dreaming will always arise from one of these three areas. Some dreams are spiritual, others are soulish or emotional in nature like a past memory that went awry, and still others may deal with some aspect of our bodies. We may dream about being shot or hurt, which may be God trying to warn us about something. We can pray, submit our dreams to God, and be educated by God while our conscious minds are shut down and our bodies are sleeping. Tell the Lord you want to dedicate your dream life to Him.

I wonder how many times God has tried to warn us through our dreams, but our minds were so filled with brain chatter we couldn't hear Him. Whatever you fill your mind with, fill it with the Word of God. Be proactive about what you feed your mind. Create an atmosphere for God to work through your dreams. Desire to center your entire being on the Lord. The Spirit of God descended and rested on Jesus (see John 1:32). We also need the Spirit of God to rest on us, and not just visit us.

MEDITATION

Meditation can also affect *what* and *how* we dream. Meditation has received a bad reputation lately because the term is often used by New Age practitioners. However, meditation on the Lord or on the Bible is quite biblical and predates New Age by a longshot.

"This Book of the Law shall not depart from your mouth; but you shall meditate in it day and night, that you may observe to do according to all that is written in it. For then you will make your way prosperous, and then you will have good success" (Joshua 1:8).

By meditating on God's Word, it begins to roll over and over in our thoughts, so it can penetrate our conscious and subconscious minds and even come alive in our dreams.

What we meditate on will impact our dreams. **"In His law he meditates day and night" (see Psalm 1:2).** If you fear not being able to pay your bills, that is what you will dream about. Whatever you fear, you will dream about. Our minds and thoughts must be grounded in the Word of God and the Spirit of God to overcome fear.

Don't just read a chapter or two a day; focus on the Word until it comes alive in you. You may have a stronghold of fear from a spirit of fear, but when God's Word comes alive in you, everything else becomes unimportant. **"For God has not given us a spirit of fear, but of power and of love and of a sound mind." (2 Timothy 1:7).**

Fear can also penetrate our conscious and subconscious minds and come alive in our dreams. If you're always thinking about your business and what you must do, this will disturb your sleep and impact your dream life. Take control of your thoughts before your fear grips you and takes control of you and your dreams.

VISIONS

A vision is basically a dream we have while we're awake. Visions can come in the form of mental pictures or open visions that we see physically. John's experience on the Isle of Patmos was a vision that became Scripture. We see pictures of beasts with multiple heads and other creatures that could represent various things.

In the Old Testament, the Hebrew word for "vision" is *hazon*, which is used three ways in Scripture as: 1) a means of direct revelation, 2) a message received by prophetic revelation, or 3) a written message received by a prophet.

In the New Testament, the Greek word for "vision" is *chazon*, which means a mental sight, picture, revelation, oracle, or prophecy. Isaiah, Ezekiel, Daniel, and the apostle John were just some of the men who had visions recorded in Scripture.

Visions can be mental pictures or movies, or open visions that we see with our physical eyes and not just our minds. When a word from the Lord is not received audibly, it can come in the form of a picture, movie, or vision.

TRANCES

Trances are similar to visions but are received while in a state of suspended voluntary movement and unconsciousness. Trances sometimes occur after advanced periods of meditation or waiting on the Lord. One New Testament example of a trance is in Acts 10.

> **The next day, as they went on their journey and drew near the city, Peter went up on the housetop to pray, about the sixth hour. Then he became very hungry and wanted to eat; but while they made ready, he fell into a trance and saw heaven opened and an object like a great sheet bound at the four corners, descending to him and let down to the earth. In it were all kinds of four-footed animals of the earth, wild beasts, creeping things, and birds of the air. And a voice came to him, "Rise, Peter; kill and eat."**
>
> **But Peter said, "Not so, Lord! For I have never eaten anything common or unclean."**
>
> **And a voice spoke to him again the second time, "What God has cleansed you must not call common." This was done three times. And the object was taken up into heaven again (Acts 10:9-16).**

The apostle Peter was in an intense time of prayer and fasting when he fell into the trance. After the trance, he spent the rest of Acts 10 processing the prophetic. We all tend to process revelation through our prophetic filters—dreams, visions, impressions, trances, or words from the Lord. In my own life, I know there has been a dramatic increase in what the Lord has been showing me, which has included a great element of teaching.

Many people don't experience visions and dreams until they're told they are available to them. They only know and believe what their religious background taught them. The mere fact that you are reading this book tells me you are spiritually, mentally, and emotionally mature enough to receive such teachings and experiences. There are deep truths in the Word of God just waiting to be unearthed in this hour.

God speaks more than we realize. He will try multiple ways to communicate revelation to us. Sometimes we think it's just our thoughts, but the Holy Spirit can speak through our thoughts. God is Spirit and spirits don't have vocal cords, so learning to distinguish our thoughts from His is one of the most valuable lessons we can learn in this life.

It's important to learn to distinguish the voice of God from the voices of demons as well, because they can also sound like thoughts. Evil thoughts can come from demons. God instructs us through images, pictures, and emotions to turn us from our deeds and suppress our pride. Through visions and dreams of the night, God can keep us from the pit, from perishing by the sword, from messing up, from bad relationships, and much more. He can even turn us from evil deeds and prevent us from killing ourselves.

The seer realm is about receiving mental images and movies. Jesus said while on earth that He only did what He saw the Father doing (see John 5:19). He had to see and hear the Father to act. Jesus had the seer ability, which is reserved for God's sons and daughters. This is among our most important duties as Christians —to accurately hear the voice of God. God has much to say about big things and small.

THE GIFTS OF THE HOLY SPIRIT

We must desire the full restoration of all the gifts of the Spirit. Though they're not all revelatory gifts, all the gifts partner with the prophetic. Below are the nine gifts of the Spirit listed in 1 Corinthians 12 with brief definitions.

The following three gifts of the Spirit enable us to *think* like God:

1. A word of knowledge—supernatural knowledge of things past or present in the natural world.

2. Discerning of spirits—supernatural ability to determine the motivating spirit behind words or actions in specific situations, whether human, evil, or divine.

3. A word of wisdom—supernatural ability to apply acquired knowledge to a given situation that brings about the desired outcome, or results in God's will being done.

The following three gifts of the Spirit enable us to *act* like God:

4. The gift of faith—God's faith imparted to us, so we can believe for the supernatural. This exceeds the measure of faith all humans possess, which is enough faith for salvation.

5. Gifts of healings—supernatural, gradual, and progressive restoration of health to man's spirit, soul, and body.

6. The working of miracles—momentary, instantaneous works of God that produce results that defy the laws of nature.

The following three gifts of the Spirit enable us to *speak* like God:

7. Different kinds of tongues—supernatural utterances or ability to speak in other languages unknown to the speaker. In personal prayer settings, the individual's spirit speaks to God without the mind needing to know the meaning. In church settings, a message is given to the church in which one, two, or at the most three, speak aloud in other languages under the Spirit's inspiration, then another interprets it so all may understand and benefit.

8. Interpretation of tongues—the interpreted theme of a message given in unknown tongues or languages. This is not an exact translation, but a general interpretive theme provided by the Holy Spirit.

9. Prophecy—a supernatural exhortation that is uplifting and encouraging. This includes speaking and preaching under inspiration of the Holy Spirit and writing history before it happens. Prophecy can be both foretelling and forthtelling.

FRUIT BEFORE GIFTS

The nine gifts of the Spirit are supernatural tools to help us win the lost, build the church, and defeat the works of darkness. Not coincidentally, there are nine fruit of the Spirit to balance these nine gifts. What good is the gift of prophecy without the fruit of meekness? Everyone would brag about their gifting. Many people are interested in the gifts of the Spirit but not as many are interested in the fruit of the Spirit. I truly believe that gifted people who lack the fruit of the Spirit are among the biggest dangers to the church, because they lack the needed character to sustain the gifts. The gifts and callings of God *are* irrevocable, meaning God doesn't give them, then take them back. However, if our fruit is not commensurate with our gifts, our gifts will not accomplish what they should. Proverbs 18:16 says, **"A man's gift makes room for him and brings him before great men."**

It was said of Jesus: **"God anointed Jesus of Nazareth with the Holy Spirit and with power, who went about doing good and healing all who were oppressed by the devil, for God was with Him"** (see Acts 10:38).

Notice Jesus went about **"doing good *and* healing all who were oppressed by the devil."** This speaks first of His character, quality, fruit, and goodness as a person before it mentions His spiritual gift of healing. Jesus did "good" and that came before healings and workings of miracles. If we're to follow Jesus' example, we should pursue the *fruit* of the Spirit, so we can be entrusted with the *gifts* of the Spirit.

THE DEMONSTRATION OF THE SPIRIT

No doubt, the early church operated and functioned in the gifts of the Spirit to further prove their ministry to those who listened to them. The book of Acts describes the actions of the apostles. However, one could easily argue the book actually describes the actions of the Holy Spirit. What would Acts be without the demonstration of the Holy Spirit and His gifts? Can you imagine Acts without these gifts?

Can you imagine Acts 2 without tongues of fire; Acts 3 without the lame man being healed at the gate called Beautiful; Acts 4 without the house shaking after they prayed, or Acts 8 without Phillip doing miracles in Samaria? What about Saul of Tarsus in Acts 9 without his supernatural experience on the road to Damascus that left him blind and needing healing through Ananias? Or Acts 10 where Peter fell in a trance after prayer and fasting, which gave him supernatural direction for spreading the gospel to non-Jewish peoples? On and on we could go, but ultimately what makes Acts special is the gifts of the Spirit in the church which confirmed the apostles' preaching and teaching and demonstrated the power of God to broken and fallen humanity.

> **"And my speech and my preaching were not with persuasive words of human wisdom, but in demonstration of the Spirit and of power: that your faith should not stand in the wisdom of men but in the power of God" (1 Corinthians 2:4-5).**

Paul said the key to his effectiveness was not oratory skills, advanced psychology, flashy titles, or stomping and snorting as he preached but the demonstration of the Spirit and power. Oh, that we would have a true renewal of spiritual gifts in the true church of the living God! So many Bible stories we read are unique because of the supernatural displays of God's power in everyday situations and circumstances. Most of the healings Jesus performed were not done in the synagogues or for the religious elite. Most of His miracles happened where people lived and worked—not in church services, general councils, or camp meetings but on street corners, beside wells, in homes, at weddings, or at funerals.

I wonder how many miracles and demonstrations of the Spirit we would see if we employed the gifts of the Spirit outside our church services. The truth is most of the gifts of the Spirit we see today happen in church services. The fact that we are *not* employing the gifts for the same purposes or in the same places Jesus and the apostles did could be hindering and holding back an increase in the gifts of the Spirit. We have become really good at praying for each other in church services, but when was the last time we saw a miracle happen at a wedding where people were celebrating, at a graveyard where people were mourning, or on a street corner where a blind man was begging?

The Holy Spirit is just as powerful today as He was in the first century for the Messiah and apostles. Could it be that the supernatural power we desire is waiting for us to exercise our faith and giftings in new places and among new people? Could it be that we are seeking reactions instead of results?

In twenty-plus years of ministry, I have ministered in camp meetings and at conferences and fellowship meetings across this nation. I certainly do not claim to have seen the results that some, with lasting legacies, have seen. However, I have seen hundreds of people baptized with the Holy Spirit. I have personally witnessed blind eyes and deaf ears being opened. I have been in meetings where I have ministered to total strangers and God has given me words of knowledge and wisdom and intricate details about their lives for the purpose of building their faith, just as Jesus did with the woman at the well (see John 4:7-19). I have been allowed to know and tell secret plans and discussions that I recounted by revelation from the Lord.

One unique gifting I regularly receive is to know and reveal details of prophetic dreams with prophetic interpretations. I certainly have not seen miracles in every service. In fact, there have been many times I was frustrated because I did *not* see the level of manifestations I desired. However, I have seen incredible miracles performed, and one thing they all had in common was the level of expectation in those places. There was an intense focus on God through increased prayer and fasting. Sure, there were some miracles where headaches were relieved, and colds were subdued. No miracle should be minimized, but I am mostly speaking of notable miracles done by a supernatural hand that no one can deny.

Prayer is the key that opens the door. I truly believe when our days and services begin with focused and intense prayer, this creates an atmosphere that invokes the supernatural power of Almighty God. Fasting is another key. Fasting is not about earning supernatural power; it's about getting the flesh out of the way, so the gifts that reside in us can come out of us. Fasting moves us more than God. It removes the layers that hinder the release of the Spirit of God in us, like peeling off onion layers until we reach the core where the scent and potency is strongest.

This end-time truth with which we have been entrusted needs to be accompanied by the gifts of the Holy Spirit. Remember, the combination of spirit and truth brings results (see John 4:24). Also remember, we don't follow signs; signs follow us (see Mark 16:17, 20). Nothing validates our covenant apostolic message more than the gifts of the Spirit.

"Lord, give us the desire to pray and fast until we are taken to a new level of power with God." Finally, remember we cannot pray or fast enough to earn God's love, but we *can* consecrate ourselves to the point that we receive God's favor (see Joel 2:15-19). We cannot earn God's love, but we *can* receive His blessings and favor. Always strive to function in the genuine gifts of the Holy Spirit.

> **So then, after the Lord had spoken to them, He was received up into heaven, and sat down at the right hand of God. And they went out and preached everywhere, the Lord working with them and confirming the word through the accompanying signs. Amen. (Mark 16:19-20).**

DISCUSSION QUESTIONS

1. Name some of the ways God speaks.

2. In your own words, define a dream. Then, explain some of the benefits of dreams (See Job 33:16-18).

3. What percentage of dreams are literal? Symbolic?

4. Think or share about a recent short dream you had. Ask the Lord or the group to interpret it for you. Was the interpretation helpful? Explain.

5. What are some lessons we can learn from Joseph's dream about him and his brothers? (interpretation, sharing with others, etc.)

6. How can meditating on the Lord or on the Word of God affect our dreams? Why is this important?

7. In your own words, define a vision. How are visions different from dreams?

8. Have someone in the group share a vision they had. What was that like?

9. Share with the group an experience involving one of the gifts of the Holy Spirit. Maybe God did something supernatural through you to help someone else, or maybe you were on the receiving end of the gift.

10. Pray and ask God to give you at least one gift of the Holy Spirit to help others. Also ask Him which gift that might be (see 1 Corinthians 12:8-10; Romans 12:6-8; Ephesians 4:11).

"Jesus characteristically revealed Himself
in the glory of His resurrection to lowly,
unknown, undistinguished people."

PASSION FOR
the Prophetic

"Behold, I stand at the door and knock. If anyone hears My voice and opens the door, I will come in to him and dine with him, and he with Me. To him who overcomes I will grant to sit with Me on My throne, as I also overcame and sat down with My Father on His throne" (Revelation 3:20-21).

On July 24, 1998, I preached my very first sermon from this verse. Little did I know then how this passage would continue to unfold and bring more revelation to my life. The Lord desires to manifest Himself and commune with us even more than we want Him to. When I began ministering at age thirteen, there was just something about this verse that called out to me.

In the Bible, these words are printed in red ink because they are the words of our Lord Jesus speaking to the church of Laodicea. The parallels between the modern church and Laodicean church of the New Testament have always astounded me. This was the seventh and final church of Asia Minor to which Jesus personally delivered this message. Strikingly, it was the only church about whose spiritual state He did not have much good to say.

Still, after He lovingly chastened them regarding their lukewarm state, there was a redemptive nature to His rebuke.

That is the difference between chastening and punishing. Punishing only punishes. Chastening has a fatherly correction to it for the purpose of bettering the conditions and lives of those being chastened. It is not just punishment for the sake of punishment.

In Revelation 3:20, the Lord gave us several keys to respond in repentance and draw near to Him. This call went out to a church that had not received much good news from the Lord about their spiritual condition. Notice the unique wording of this verse shows us the proper way to approach the Lord and commune with Him. AOPRRC is the acronym for this scriptural approach:

Attention - "Behold, I stand at the door and knock."
Opportunity - "If anyone"
Perception - "hears"
Recognition - "My voice"
Response - "and opens the door"
Communion - "I will come in to him and dine with him."

RESPONDING TO HIS INVITATION

If we respond to His call and give Him our <u>attention</u>, He will give us an <u>opportunity</u> to <u>perceive</u> and <u>recognize</u> His voice and <u>respond</u> to Him. The result of this will be His manifest presence in <u>communion</u>. His sheep know His voice (see John 10:4). By spending time getting to know Him, we will recognize His voice. No one can adequately teach us to recognize the sound of His voice, but once we hear it, we'll know it. I wonder how many times the Lord has made Himself available to us like in Revelation 3:20 but we never responded. Despite our spiritual condition, He never stops knocking.

"Behold, I stand at the door and knock." How many times has the Lord been as close as a knock away? What if Moses hadn't turned aside to see the burning bush? Israel could have remained slaves longer than necessary, thanks to Moses's inability to give the Lord his <u>attention</u> in that moment. How many times have we dreamed, heard our names spoken at night, felt an impression, or had two or three people bring up the same subject in succession yet passed them all off as coincidences? Did we give due <u>attention</u> to what the Lord wanted to reveal?

"If anyone…" Yes, this means all of us. How incredible that the God of creation thinks about us. His thoughts about us are numerous (see Psalm 139:17) and He calls whosoever will (see Revelation 22:17). This is our <u>opportunity</u>.

"Hears my voice…" Hebrews 5:14 says, **"But solid food belongs to those who are of full age, that is, those who by reason of use have their senses exercised to discern both good and evil."** Now more than ever the church needs to be trained and equipped to develop its spiritual senses by practicing the art of seeing, hearing, tasting, smelling, and touching the Lord.

This is why there is so much grace on the prophetic message. When we recognize that God is speaking and wants to make Himself known, we'll want as many as possible to develop their senses to hear His voice. This is why spiritual <u>perception</u> and <u>recognition</u> are so important.

"And opens the door…" In what ways can we <u>respond</u> to the Lord? What gentle nudges have we ignored and then become frustrated because the Lord never shared any big revelation with us"? Perhaps we can start by responding to the Lord in simple ways, like stopping and praying no matter where we are or what we're doing when we feel His presence.

We must learn to live our lives as Jesus did, constantly waiting to see and hear what the Father is saying and doing (see John 5:19, 30). There simply is no better life than learning to do these simple things over and over until we learn to walk in the Spirit.

"I will come in to him and dine with him." Everyone wants this. We sing about it, preach about it, ask for it, but we cannot have this experience if we don't first meet the conditions He gave us in the rest of this verse. I'm not into steps or formulas. That's not what this is about. I'm simply saying Jesus shows us in this verse how to have <u>communion</u> with Him. We must accept the entirety of this verse and recognize the value of His invitation.

ON THE ROAD TO EMMAUS

The two disciples on the road to Emmaus provide another example of passion becoming a doorway to encounter and prophetic revelation.

> **Now behold, two of them were traveling that same day to a village called Emmaus, which was seven miles from Jerusalem. And they talked together of all these things which had happened. So it was, while they conversed and reasoned, that Jesus Himself drew near and went with them. But their eyes were restrained, so that they did not know Him.**
>
> **And He said to them, "What kind of conversation is this that you have with one another as you walk and are sad?" Then the one whose name was Cleopas answered and said to Him, "Are You the only stranger in Jerusalem, and have You not known the things which happened there in these days?"**
>
> **And He said to them, "What things?"**

So they said to Him, "The things concerning Jesus of Nazareth, who was a Prophet mighty in deed and word before God and all the people, and how the chief priests and our rulers delivered Him to be condemned to death, and crucified Him. But we were hoping that it was He who was going to redeem Israel. Indeed, besides all this, today is the third day since these things happened. Yes, and certain women of our company, who arrived at the tomb early, astonished us. When they did not find His body, they came saying that they had also seen a vision of angels who said He was alive. And certain of those who were with us went to the tomb and found it just as the women had said; but Him they did not see."

Then He said to them, "O foolish ones, and slow of heart to believe in all that the prophets have spoken! Ought not the Christ to have suffered these things and to enter into His glory?" And beginning at Moses and all the Prophets, He expounded to them in all the Scriptures the things concerning Himself.

Then they drew near to the village where they were going, and He indicated that He would have gone farther. But they constrained Him, saying, "Abide with us, for it is toward evening, and the day is far spent." And He went in to stay with them.

Now it came to pass, as He sat at the table with them, that He took bread, blessed and broke it, and gave it to them. Then their eyes were opened and they knew Him; and He vanished from their sight.

And they said to one another, "Did not our heart burn within us while He talked with us on the road, and while He opened the Scriptures to us?" So they rose up that very hour and returned to Jerusalem, and found the eleven and those who were with them gathered together, saying, "The Lord is risen indeed, and has appeared to Simon!" And they

told about the things that had happened on the road, and how He was known to them in the breaking of bread (Luke 24:13-35).

DON'T MISS YOUR VISITATION

After leaving the Passover celebration, these two men traveled and talked together. They were not famous apostles; they were semi-anonymous followers of Jesus. Jesus characteristically revealed Himself in the glory of His resurrection to lowly, unknown, undistinguished people. He is the Savior of the common man and often reveals and manifests Himself to unknown people.

These two believers were walking and talking together about what was heavy on their hearts. Like most people, they talked about recent events and past disappointments, and in doing so, nearly missed an opportunity for fellowship and encounter with the Lord. They were so caught up in the drama surrounding Jesus' resurrection, they nearly missed their moment to encounter the resurrected Christ.

When Jesus joined them as a third person, they neither recognized Him nor His presence. We don't fully understand *why* they didn't recognize Him, but I believe their state of mind might have affected their vision. I believe their processing over and over the bad news about losing their Savior hindered them. We need to move on from the issues *surrounding* the Savior and look *for* the Savior.

Isn't it awesome that Jesus was willing to join just two or three gathered in His name (see Matthew 18:20)? It didn't need to be a crowd. And isn't it interesting that Jesus joined them just as they started talking about Him? When they started talking about Him, Jesus drew near. God wants to appear to us more than we want

Him to appear. The atmosphere can change when we start talking about the Lord or just listen to worship or pray.

Jesus quietly listened to their conversation for a while. Their countenances were sad based on recent events. They did not know they had no reason to be sad. They asked Jesus if He knew about the recent events. As it turned out, He knew more than they did. This reminds me of times when I have asked the Lord questions. I have asked Him so many things out of ignorance. Sometimes we think we know better than Jesus. Jesus encouraged them to reveal their hearts though He knew their hearts and what they were thinking. Even though He knows, He still values us sharing with Him what's on our hearts and minds.

He skillfully played along with their conversation. They said, **"We were hoping that it was He who was going to redeem Israel."** Their hopes seemed dashed. They only knew part of the story. We see through a glass darkly. **"Hope deferred makes the heart sick" (see Proverbs 13:12).** They seemed unimpressed by Mary's testimony. They needed to experience Him for themselves. Sometimes even the most reliable testimonies of others can only help us so much. We need tangible encounters for ourselves; we need Jesus to appear to us.

Jesus said they were **"slow of heart to believe in all that the prophets have spoken."** Because they did not know the Scriptures regarding the Messiah, they had lost all hope. Jesus taught them the greatest Bible study of all time. Beginning with Moses and the Prophets, He expounded the Scriptures to them. His teaching style was expository, letting the Scriptures speak for themselves.

Jesus indicated He would have walked and talked further with them, but they had arrived at their destination. Jesus did not force Himself on them. They constrained Him to come and stay with them. Though they did not recognize Him or His presence, they wanted to spend as much time with Him as possible. They likely didn't even know *why* they were so drawn to Him. **"He took bread, blessed and broke it, and gave it to them."** Then their eyes were opened, and they knew Him, and He vanished.

Before the meal, their eyes were restrained so they did not know Him. What opened their eyes to Him? Jesus is the bread that came down from heaven (see John 6:32-33). Perhaps they were present at the feeding of the five thousand when Jesus distributed the bread. Perhaps they had somehow participated with Him and the disciples at the Last Supper four days earlier. Perhaps they saw His nail-pierced hands when He gave them the bread.

Matthew described the Last Supper: **"And as they were eating, Jesus took bread, blessed and broke it, and gave it to the disciples and said, 'Take, eat; this is My body'"** (Matthew 26:26). Four days later with these two men, Luke records: **"Now it came to pass, as He sat at the table with them, that He took bread, blessed and broke it, and gave it to them. Then their eyes were opened, and they knew Him"** (see Luke 24:30-31).

THE FELLOWSHIP OF BURNING HEARTS

Their eyes were opened when He repeated the process of the Last Supper. Our eyes can also be opened to Him in the process of breaking the bread. He revealed the process of the crucified life. Many of us have had to endure and overcome the breaking process to be blessed and become a blessing to others. Jesus was revealed in the process of the breaking of bread, and He is still revealed in that process.

Jesus could be right in front of us, sitting with us at our meals or riding in our cars, but our eyes are restrained from seeing Him.

The prayer and heart's cry of every believer should be, "Jesus, open our spiritual eyes!" Later, the two disciples said, **"Did not our hearts burn within us?"** These two men were part of the fellowship of burning hearts.

Here is yet another example of processing the prophetic. The prophetic filter through which Jesus revealed Himself to them was bread. No doubt, these disciples had just broken bread four days prior at the Passover, so Jesus took that life experience of breaking bread to bring revelation to them. Though their eyes beheld Him, and their hearts burned with passion, they still did not know Him until He used a memory or past experience to open their eyes. After Jesus broke bread, **"then their eyes were opened."** This was their prophetic filter. God uses past natural experiences, symbols, and connotations to open our spiritual eyes to encounters with Him.

After Jesus led them in a Bible study and received revelation from God's Word, after they walked and talked with the Lord and invited Him in to dine with them, their spiritual eyes were opened, and they joined the fellowship of burning hearts.

COME AND DINE WITH HIM

Dining with Jesus is a clear prophetic picture. **"Behold, I stand at the door and knock. If anyone hears My voice and opens the door, I will come in to him and dine with him, and he with Me" (Revelation 3:20).** How many times has the Lord visited us and we were unaware? Did we miss our visitation?

How many times has God been present among us, but we were so caught up reliving our past or taking a trip down "Memory Lane," we failed to check our surroundings to see if the Lord was trying to appear in that moment through nature or some other natural experience? Becoming aware of our natural surroundings is called "situational awareness." Doing this to see if God might be speaking to us through our natural surroundings is called "prophetic awareness."

Another term for our time of visitation is "*kairos* moments." *Kairos* is the Greek New Testament word for a moment in time. *Chronos* is the Greek word for chronological time. A *kairos* moment is when the spirit realm is highlighted to us, and a supernatural grace is released to us in a moment within chronological time to accomplish a kingdom purpose.

Romans 13:11 is one example of a *kairos* moment: **"And do this, knowing the time, that now it is high time to awake out of sleep; for now our salvation is nearer than when we first believed."** Paul said now, in the present, is the perfect time to wake up and see what God is doing and seize the moment.

Breaking and eating bread is not always a *kairos* moment; sometimes it's just eating bread. However, there are moments when God can reveal Himself to us and speak to us through breaking and eating bread. That moment of breaking bread was highlighted to these two men, and it became a supernatural experience. Not every time a bush burns is a man called to his destiny, but God speaking to Moses through a burning bush was another *kairos* moment when heaven invaded earth and eternity invaded time to bring revelation. Yet, without situational awareness in the moment, we can miss our prophetic revelations and *kairos* moments.

"Then Moses said, 'I will now turn aside, and see this great sight, why the bush does not burn'" (Exodus 3:3). Again, what if Moses hadn't turned aside and noticed the burning bush? I wonder how many times Moses had seen a burning bush in the hot desert before. But *this* time the bush was burning and not being consumed, and *this* time it meant something. It was a *kairos* moment and a message from God. Not every year is the Super Bowl a prophetic revelation, but some years the winner of the Super Bowl means something and knowing when it means something and when it doesn't is key.

Have you ever been awakened at night? Some believers have been awakened at night, and like Samuel, have even heard their name being called (see 1 Samuel 3:4-10). Others have awakened and felt a hand touch them. Yet how many times do we just turn over and go back to sleep? The Lord wants to come in and make His abode with us.

Jesus was made known to these two men in the process of breaking bread. Their eyes were opened when they invited Him into their house and sat to dine with Him. The Lord has shown me that too many people's understanding of God, and even their theology, whether spoken or written, prevents their eyes from being opened. Just think how many books and commentaries have been written about the Word of God that place doubts in our minds about what we should and should not expect from God.

The two men who met Jesus on the road to Emmaus were not famous apostles. Only one of them—Cleopas—is even named in the story, and that is all we know about him. Our theological minds have no problem believing Christ would reveal Himself to someone like Peter or John, but to a couple of nameless nobodies? These two men are evidence that God is no respecter of persons (see Acts 10:34) and that we do not need to be well-known speakers, preachers, intercessors, or prophets for the Lord Jesus to take a personal interest in us and come dine with us. This is good news!

In the Middle East today, radical Muslims are experiencing dreams and encounters with the Lord. And once they encounter

Him, no one has to preach to them or try to convince them about Him. How many times has the Lord wanted to appear to us, or bring words of knowledge or angelic encounters to us, but because we didn't learn to harness our thoughts or remained in a state of depression, we were blinded to these spiritual realities?

This goes beyond head knowledge or theology. Our theology can only go so far with people. We need more than oral presentations; we need to preach through the greater works of Christ. Will we be the ones who preach through the greater works of Christ? I believe there is coming a company of believers who will experience the Lord more than the initial outpouring at Pentecost.

This eating and dining with Jesus is a prophetic picture. Jesus reveals Himself through this process. The Lord desires to dwell with us and promises to dine with us. This idea of the Lord dining with His people is not a foreign concept. The Lord ate with the seventy elders of Israel on the mountain of God (see Exodus 24:9-11). The Lord dined with these two men in Emmaus (see Luke 24:30), and the Lord frequently dined with His disciples both before and after His resurrection (see Matthew 8:14, 9:10; Luke 24:41-43; John 21:12-3).

WAIT ON THE LORD

Psalm 119:55 says, **"I remember Your name in the night, O Lord, and I keep Your law."** If you want to know how to sit and wait on the Lord at night, stop counting sheep and start counting your blessings. This concept of seeking the Lord at night is also important. Kenneth Hagin often sat up at night waiting for the Lord to visit him. The Lord finally visited him and asked him, "Why have you been sitting up at night?" Hagin said, "Lord, I wanted to sit up to keep You company because most of the saints are asleep." The Lord appeared to him because of the sincerity of his heart.

Psalm 37:7 says, **"Rest in the Lord, and wait patiently for Him."** The word **"rest"** here is the Hebrew word *damam*, which means to be silent. So, cease from striving within, hold your peace, quiet yourself, and wait. Psalm 40:1 says, **"I waited patiently for the Lord; and He inclined to me, and heard my cry."** Waiting requires quiet endurance. We must condition our spirits before He visits. The impatient restlessness of our humanity must be subdued in us. Isaiah 64:4 says, **"You, Who acts for the one who waits for Him."** God not only works on behalf of those who wait for Him, but He also does a work of preparation for those who wait. God works while we wait.

Proverbs 8:34 says, **"Blessed is the man who listens to me, watching daily at my gates, waiting at the posts of my doors."** This practice and discipline of waiting must be daily. Lamentations 3:24-25 says, **"'The Lord is my portion,' says my soul, 'Therefore I hope in Him!' The Lord is good to those who wait for Him, to the soul who seeks Him."** We must learn to wait and anticipate His arrival saying, "If not today, perhaps tomorrow."

Psalm 42:1-2 says, **"As the deer pants after the water brooks, so pants my soul for You, O God. My soul thirsts for God, for the living God. When shall I come and appear before God?"** Hosea 6:3 says, **"His going forth is established as the morning; He will come to us like the rain, like the latter and former rain to the earth."** Hosea said the Lord appearing to those who wait for Him is as sure as the rising of the sun in the morning and the coming of the rainy seasons. Finally, Isaiah 30:18 says, **"Blessed are all those who wait for Him."** Shut down all distractions, and He will visit you as you wait for Him. Make this your prayer: "Father, I want to know You experientially."

Two basic questions for processing the prophetic are: "What is God trying to say to me?" and "How should I respond?" Learning to recognize significant *kairos* moments in our lives and then taking the appropriate actions are two of the most important qualities any prophetic person can have.

Now after John was put in prison, Jesus came to Galilee, preaching the gospel of the kingdom of God, and saying, "The time is fulfilled, and the kingdom of God is at hand. Repent, and believe in the gospel."

And as He walked by the Sea of Galilee, He saw Simon and Andrew his brother casting a net into the sea; for they were fishermen. Then Jesus said to them, "Follow Me, and I will make you become fishers of men." They immediately left their nets and followed Him (Mark 1:14-18).

KAIROS MOMENTS IN CHRONOS TIME

Kairos is one of two words the ancient Greeks used for "time." *Chronos* was the other. *Chronos* refers to a chronological timeline or sequential time; *Kairos* signifies the proper or opportune time for action. *Chronos* is quantitative in nature; *kairos* is qualitative in nature. *Kairos* also means "opportunity" or "the fitting time." The Bible uses *kairos* in numerous places in the New Testament, such as in Luke 19:44, **"because you did not know the time of your visitation,"** and in Acts 24:25 when Felix said to Paul, **"Go away for now; when I have a convenient time I will call for you."**

Jesus' first recorded sermon in Mark 1:15 is another perfect example of a *kairos* moment: **"The time is fulfilled, and the kingdom of God is at hand. Repent, and believe in the gospel."** Aren't you glad the disciples responded correctly to their *kairos* moment? The Israelites who lived in Jesus' day were also confronted with Jesus' ministry and message. They also had a *kairos* opportunity and responsibility to respond appropriately, but they did not.

> **Now as He drew near, He saw the city and wept over it, saying, "If you had known, even you, especially in this your day, the things that make for your peace! But now they are hidden from your eyes. For days will come upon you when your enemies will build an embankment around you, surround you and close you in on every side, and level you, and your children within you, to the ground; and they will not leave in you one stone upon another, because you did not know the time of your visitation" (Luke 19:41-44).**

Here we clearly see the significance of a divine moment or season, and the consequences we can experience over time by not responding correctly to our *kairos* moment. Much of the first-century Jewish community rejected Christ as their Messiah, and Jesus explained the consequences of this were completely tied to them missing their *kairos* moment. He told them their entire temple would be destroyed and their oppressors would surround and destroy their city and their entire system of worship.

He then explained *why* they would experience this: because they missed the time of their visitation. Though they were physically present in the time of their visitation, their hearts and lives were not aligned with God's purpose for that moment in history. In other words, they did not seize the moment or opportunity by recognizing Jesus as their Messiah. The result would be the destruction of Jerusalem in AD 70, when more than a million Jews were killed and nearly that same amount were taken as slaves. The consequence of missing their moment in time would be their entire city and culture being destroyed. Israel would not exist as a nation for another 1,900 years.

Likewise, when Jesus called Simon Peter and Andrew to follow Him, they also had a window of opportunity to leave all and follow Christ or stay with their fishing nets. Fishing was their trade. They had been commercial fishermen for years, so they knew the ins and outs of the trade and relied on that income to support their families. It was no small thing for them to walk away from financial and economic security and a reliable job that provided for their families with a simple glance and a few words, yet there was so much grace on that moment when Jesus simply said, **"Follow Me."** Perhaps it was the look in His eye, or the anointing and life-giving power of His words. Something happened in that moment that demanded a response.

They did more than respond; they were willing to change the course of their lives and rely on God to provide for them. By seizing that moment in time, their lives were forever changed. In fact, many of the stories and books of the New Testament were written by another man who responded correctly to his *kairos* moment when it came, namely Paul. We too can truly begin to sense God's purpose, presence, and destiny in our daily lives when we become consciously aware of these moments of possibility. Once we gain the spiritual discernment and sensitivity to recognize these moments, we can begin to respond daily, process the prophetic, and cooperate with God's purpose for our lives.

In the New Testament, *kairos* means the appointed time of God's purpose or the time when God acts. In Mark 1:15, *kairos* was fulfilled, and the kingdom of God was at hand. *Kairos* is used eighty-six times in the New Testament. It refers to the opportune time, moment, or season, such as harvest time.

Chronos is used fifty-four times and refers to a specific amount of time, such as a day or an hour. For example, **"Now for a *time* of about forty years He put up with their ways in the wilderness"** (Acts 13:18, emphasis added), and **"Now when much *time* had been spent, and sailing was now dangerous"** (see Acts 27:9, emphasis added). In John 7:6, Jesus made a clear distinction between His *kairos* time to go to Jerusalem, which had

"not yet come," and His brothers' *chronos* time to go to Jerusalem, which was **"always ready."** They could go to Jerusalem any *chronos* time they wished, whereas He could only go to Jerusalem at the *kairos* time.

Kairos means opportunity or "opportune time." It is derived from the Greek word *kara*, which means "head," referring to things "coming to a head." It means to seize or take full advantage of the moment. *Kairos* can also mean the right, suitable, or favorable moment.

DON'T MISS YOUR KAIROS MOMENT

Esther faced just such a moment when she boldly turned toward great opposition which threatened not only her own life but also all of Israel. In this moment, she courageously said, **"My maids and I will fast likewise. And so I will go to the king, which is against the law; and if I perish, I perish!"** (see Esther **4:16)** Esther understood it was her *kairos* moment to boldly face great opposition. She knew she had come to the kingdom **"for a such a time as this"** (see Esther **4:14).**

What if Moses had missed his *kairos* moment at the burning bush? He abandoned the desert and sheep to give God his undivided attention, and because he did, two million people were delivered from bondage and slavery.

The two men on the road to Emmaus nearly missed their *kairos* moment. After Jesus shared with them the Scriptures concerning the Messiah and broke bread with them, He was suddenly made known to them just before vanishing out of sight. What if the woman at the well had missed her *kairos* moment? It was just another day at the well. She was a Samaritan; Jesus was a

Jew. She was a woman; He was a man. Yet, she seized her moment by letting Him speak into her life.

The Lord will establish us and put us in geographical places where we can be planted and bloom. Sometimes He will reorder our steps. Other times our *kairos* moments will be predetermined. Still other times God will use us to facilitate someone else's *kairos* moment. God will even sanction *kairos* moments in places like Brownsville and Azusa Street. When we enter significant *kairos* moments in our lives, we should not hesitate. However, don't look back and kick yourself because you didn't seize your *kairos* moment when Jesus said, **"Follow Me."**

Throughout Scripture and history, we can see the importance of taking advantage of divine moments and seasons. We can also clearly see the consequences for not responding correctly to those *kairos* moments. Sometimes, even the slightest hesitation can result in a missed opportunity. Other times, God gives us second, third, and even fourth chances, especially for those He has marked, chosen, commissioned, or ordained to become world changers, reformers, or movers and shakers.

We as a church and as individuals are stepping into a season and a moment of destiny right now in which God is connecting us with the right people in our lives. Some are relocating. Others are being ordained and recommissioned. Still others are stepping up and recognizing God's purpose for this moment. When you know God is giving you a grace to do something, do it with all your heart. Don't miss your *kairos* moments in *chronos* time.

DISCUSSION QUESTIONS

1. What does the acronym "AOPRRC" stand for?

2. Was there a moment in your life when you felt the Lord "knocking" or trying to get your attention? How did you know? What did you do?

3. Why do you think the eyes of the two men on the road to Emmaus were restrained from seeing Jesus?

4. How and why do you think these two men's eyes were opened? Explain.

5. After their eyes were opened, the two men said, "Did not our heart burn within us?" (see Luke 24:32) What do you think they meant by that? Explain.

6. What does the "prophetic picture" of Jesus coming and dining with us mean? Explain.

7. Name some of the scriptural benefits of "waiting" on or for the Lord.

8. In light of these benefits, why do you think more people *don't* wait on the Lord? What might change their minds?

9. Describe a specific *kairos* moment or opportunity in your past. Did you seize or miss the moment? What happened? What did you learn?

10. Do you believe we are living in another *kairos* moment for the church and our nation? What do you believe God is saying to you personally about this?

"He wants to reveal His deep secrets to those who have allowed His life to truly become their own."

PERCEIVING
the Prophetic

"But we all, with unveiled face, beholding as in a mirror the glory of the Lord, are being transformed into the same image from glory to glory" (2 Corinthians 3:18).

Here, Paul wrote that, by beholding the Lord, we are being transformed from glory to glory into Christ's image. The key here is to understand "beholding," so His life can become a reality in us. *Beholding* here means a true spiritual seeing or perceiving by the Spirit's inward witness that reveals the new life of Christ in the believer. This process involves His life increasing in us, while our soul or self-life decreases. The Spirit of God will often present choices to us in real-life situations. These choices often determine who will rise up in us—the Christ life or the soul or self-life.

HE MUST INCREASE, I MUST DECREASE

When we let Christ manifest Himself in us, instead of attempting to become like Him through our human striving, our inward man will truly become more like Him. Otherwise, we will remain unchanged and untransformed. This has been the practical side of our journey since we received Christ as the seed of new life (see 1 Peter 1:23). Unfortunately, few Christians recognize this inward working, and consequently few Christians become like Christ. He remains only a seed in them, and they never develop the abundant life that Jesus promised.

We must understand our need for Him to crush our souls or self-life during our trials of faith and our great need for Him to divide our soul life from His spiritual life (see Hebrews 4:12). Essentially, there are two lives at work within us. The first is the fallen Adam, the soul life, that is our natural birth identity. The new life is Christ in us, not us trying to be like Him, but Him as our life springing forward.

The battle between our soul and spirit is ongoing, and recognizing who's who and which is which, is vastly important. Most Christians today are trying to be Christians through soul power—their mind, will, and emotions. This is an affront to the inward cross that was applied to our first fallen life. It's not about our lives being made better but our lives and our identities being found in Christ's death and burial, so He may become our only life. Christianity is in the person of Christ, but His church has predominantly ceased to be His testimony of the Spirit life.

In John 6:47-71, the Lord Jesus gave us a revelation of Himself as the manna God has forever given—the living bread from heaven—not the bread that decays when we store it. He declared Himself the bread of life and said that, unless we eat of Him, like we eat natural bread to sustain natural life, we have no life in us (see John 6:53). Our spiritual life comes from partaking of Him, who both provides and sustains life in the Spirit.

Our daily diets are important. However, the first and most basic element of life is His light. Photosynthesis occurs in plants due to light, not heat. Plants have life because of light. They even move, grow, and constantly reposition themselves to reach the light of life. Again, He said, **"I am the light of the world. He who follows Me shall not walk in darkness, but have the light of life" (see John 8:12).** John writes that Jesus came as light, but that men loved darkness instead (see John 3:19). So, both light and life are inseparable from life in the Spirit.

Jesus is the "I AM" of God (see Exodus 3:14). Seven times, Jesus declared Himself the "I AM" of the Old Testament now come in the flesh. Now may be the best time and the best place to allow Him to reveal Himself to us as "I AM." I have found that fixing my eyes on Jesus, the author and finisher of my faith, my beginning and my end, has been huge (see Hebrews 12:2). This demands my intention and attention to look to Jesus when so many other things are competing for my time, yet He is *worth* my time, attention, and devotion.

THE CHRIST LIFE

The Scriptures speak much of this Christ life—a life of living, being, doing, teaching, and ministering—all by the Spirit. **"And this is the testimony: that God has given us eternal life, and this life is in His Son. He who has the Son has life; he who does not have the Son of God does not have life" (1 John 5:11-12).** For us to realize God's complete purpose and plan, including all His eternal thoughts, God first had to put Himself, His Son, as life inside us. God's eternal intentions cannot be grasped through our natural, soulish lives. God's spiritual, eternal, and full measured intentions can only be realized by the beautiful takeover of Christ in us as our only life.

By the law of the Spirit of life in Christ Jesus (see Romans 8:2), He internally frees those who are willing to be free from their earthly life and identity. Sadly, few find Christ as their only life (see Matthew 7:14). With these days of darkness and difficulties upon us, we must allow Him to become greater within as our new life in Him, which is really just Him standing in and through us. Otherwise, we will fail to withstand in the evil day (see Ephesians 6:13).

"I have been crucified with Christ; it is no longer I who live, but Christ lives in me; and the life which I now live in the flesh I live by faith in the Son of God, who loved me and gave Himself for me" (Galatians 2:20). We must apply the way of the cross of Christ, which leads to the fullness of Christ, as our one and only life. The cross is the great divide, showing all to be in one of three categories: 1) those who do not have Christ as their inward life, 2) those who have the Christ way of life as the initial seed within, and 3) those who are moving and pressing on in Christ as their new life. The Christ life must overcome the former life with its fallen self-nature until the self-life in us no longer lives, but only Christ Himself lives His new life in us.

When He increasingly becomes that new inward life, He will indeed live in and through us. Life will simply manifest itself; life will live according to its nature, whether it is the Christ life or the soulish self-life. Each flower has a life of its own kind, which it proudly displays. So, if Christ is the fullness of God's own kind, then my choice is for Him to increase in me. **"As He is, so are we in this world" (see 1 John 4:17).** Make this your prayer: "Show Yourself, Lord, as Your life in and through me, as Your vessel. Let Your life continue to rise and dwell within me and manifest Your nature in me."

When we remember that life and light are directly connected, we realize we are following the God of revelation. He wants to reveal His deep secrets to those who have allowed His life to truly become their own. Truly, the way to grow in the prophetic is to allow His life to become ours. Just as with photosynthesis, the plant follows the light wherever it goes. **"But if we walk in the light as He is in the light, we have fellowship with one another, and the blood of Jesus Christ His Son cleanses us from all sin" (1 John 1:7).**

SPIRIT SPEAKS TO SPIRIT

To be His hands and feet, we must see ourselves as His instruments. Whatever we prophesy must be to edify the body and produce fruit in both our lives and in the lives of those to whom we prophesy. Increasing or enlarging our spirit's capacity comes from the foundation of hearing from God and properly preparing ourselves.

But we speak the wisdom of God in a mystery, the hidden wisdom which God ordained before the ages for our glory, which none of the rulers of this age knew; for had they known, they would not have crucified the Lord of glory.

But as it is written: "Eye has not seen, nor ear heard, nor have entered into the heart of man the things which God has prepared for those who love Him."

But God has revealed them to us through His Spirit. For the Spirit searches all things, yes, the deep things of God. For what man knows the things of a man except the spirit of the man which is in him? Even so no one knows the things of God except the Spirit of God. Now we have received, not the spirit of the world, but the Spirit who is from God, that we might know the things that have been freely given to us by God.

These things we also speak, not in words which man's wisdom teaches but which the Holy Spirit teaches, comparing spiritual things with spiritual. But the natural man does not receive the things of the Spirit of God, for they are foolishness to him; nor can he know them, because they are spiritually discerned. But he who is spiritual judges all things, yet he himself is rightly judged by no one. For "who has known the mind of the Lord that he may instruct Him?" But we have the mind of Christ (1 Corinthians 2:7-16).

Spiritual things are received in our spirits. If our spirits are underdeveloped, we cannot receive the things of God. We must develop our spirits to receive the words of God. He is speaking more than our ears are willing to hear and more than our spirits can receive. Spiritual things are not taught but caught by our spirits. If all we do is live natural, carnal lives, we cannot receive the things of the Spirit of God, because they are spiritually discerned.

SANCTIFIED SPIRIT, SOUL, AND BODY

The Holy Spirit in us can be no bigger than our spirits. He can be no bigger in us than the place we give Him. Enlarging our spirits' capacities is what allows the Holy Spirit to be big in us. We must spend time developing our spirits. 1 Thessalonians 5:23 says, **"Now may the God of peace Himself sanctify you completely; and may your whole spirit, soul, and body be preserved blameless at the coming of our Lord Jesus Christ."**

You are a three-part being. If you draw three circles, each inside the other, your spirit will be the inner circle, your soul the middle circle, and your body the outer circle. The Spirit of God is outside all three circles and will not enter your spirit except by invitation. But He also surrounds us, therefore everyone is surrounded by God. However, God is not *in* everyone.

The Spirit of God operates on a higher level than our spirit, and that is where faith comes in. Our spirit can search the deep things of God when we enlarge our spirit. Spirit speaks to spirit. John 4:24 says, **"God *is* Spirit,"** not *a* spirit. And if He *is* Spirit, many can be in Him. If we live soulish lives, we cannot receive the things of the Spirit of God because Spirit speaks to spirit. The more carnal and soulish we are, the more difficult it is for us to speak God's words. However, with an enlarged spirit, we can hear the deep things of God and hear His Spirit speak to our spirit.

Most of the ways God speaks to man doesn't involve sounds or vibrations. The Spirit does not have vocal cords. When spirits speak—whether God, angels, or demons—they can sound like thoughts. A person who has unnatural thoughts of suicide, revenge, or evil toward someone is hearing the voice of demons.

When He had called the people to Himself, with His disciples also, He said to them, "Whoever desires to come after Me, let him deny himself, and take up his cross, and follow Me. For whoever desires to save his life will lose it, but whoever loses his life for My sake and the gospel's will save it. For what will it profit a man if he gains the whole world, and loses his own soul? Or what will a man give in exchange for his soul? For whoever is ashamed of Me and My words in this adulterous and sinful generation, of him the Son of Man also will be ashamed when He comes in the glory of His Father with the holy angels" (Mark 8:34-38).

The single Greek word translated "soul" and "life" in these verses is *psuche*, from which we get our English word *psyche*. Our soul or mind is one of the biggest barriers to enlarging our spirits. **"The natural man does not receive the things of the Spirit of God, for they are foolishness to him; nor can he know them."** Our thought patterns can become barriers to what is in our spirit. If our worldview is contrary to the Word of God, our spirit will not agree with what the Spirit of God tries to tell us.

Our spirit can receive revelation from the Spirit of God, but then our soul or mind can block everything coming from our spirit. This is why it is so important that our spirit and soul come in agreement. Otherwise, everything in our spirit will be locked up. Our goal is to release what is in our spirit through our soul to our mouth.

I beseech you therefore, brethren, by the mercies of God, that you present your bodies a living sacrifice, holy, acceptable to God, which is your reasonable service. And do not be conformed to this world, but be transformed by the renewing of your mind, that you may prove what is that good and acceptable and perfect will of God (Romans 12:1-2).

Our body physically contains or houses our spirit and soul. Transformation takes place in our mind when our mind become subjected to the Logos—the thought, plan, idea, and Word of God. Then we can prove or demonstrate **"what is that good and acceptable and perfect will of God."**

BREAKING OUR SOUL

When we receive the thoughts of God, we can manifest those thoughts, but first we must renew our mind to think like the Bible thinks and see people through the lens or filter of God's Word. Then we can speak from the Logos of God and translate God's thoughts into reality through the Word of God. Our thoughts must never stop the Word of God from coming out of us. Spirit speaks to spirit. If we predominately live in the soulish realm (mind, will, and emotions) we cannot effectively operate in the Spirit.

Many people have stubborn souls that block their spirits from working through them. Some people are miserably saved. They still think negative, depressing thoughts because they have yet to renew their minds through the process of sanctification. God cannot effectively work through carnal-minded people. Whosoever loses his *psuche* for His sake and the gospel's will save it. (see Matthew 16:25). **"Out of his heart** [spirit] **will flow rivers of living water. But this He spoke concerning the Spirit"** **(see John 7:38-39).** Everything good comes from our spirit.

96

Healing for cancer, AIDS, and every other disease known to man resides in our spirit. The spirit knows all things and can speak about things that hinder people. The mind blocks many people from receiving the baptism in the Holy Spirit. Some people hear tongues in their minds but are afraid to utter or speak them aloud. The same is true with words of knowledge, words of wisdom, prophecy, discernment, healing, and every other gift of the Spirit. The Holy Spirit must bypass our brains to manifest. We keep the gifts of the Spirit locked up.

We also make more of impartations from others than what God intended. Other people cannot impart to us more than what we already have. We all must go through the same mind renewal process to effectively operate in the gifts. We all need the mind of Christ to work in us before the Spirit of Christ can work through us. Whosoever loses his *psuche* will save it, whoever denies himself, whoever gives up his soul-life will save it. God wants to break us. What we need in our lives is more brokenness, not more impartations.

So, what is this concept of losing our lives for the gospel's sake? If we don't break our soul, our spirit will remain locked up. God wants to make our soul like pliable tissue. Our soul needs to become an obedient servant to our spirit. If we want to release our spirit to work through us and come out of us, we must break our carnal soul. Fasting will break us. Catastrophes and suffering will break us. **"Therefore, since Christ suffered for us in the flesh, arm yourselves also with the same mind, for he who has suffered in the flesh has ceased from sin" (1 Peter 4:1).**

But we don't want to suffer. I have news for you: God does not deliver us from all tribulations. He is not trying to make our lives easier. When Jesus fasted, Satan tempted Him to turn stones into bread, but Jesus never used His giftings to gratify His flesh. Instead, He suffered and rejected fame, power, and ease from Satan. Satan is the god of this age (see 2 Corinthians 4:4). He could have given Jesus the kingdoms of this world, but Jesus did not choose the easy way out; He chose instead the sufferings of the cross.

INCREASING OUR SPIRIT'S CAPACITY

If our soul is bigger than our spirit, then we will judge people by their outward shell instead of by their inward heart (see 1 Samuel 16:7). Prophecy never speaks to people's current outward appearance; it speaks to people's potential. Spirit judges spirit. Sarai received a prophecy that she would have a baby.

When the prophetic is fully activated in our lives, we may walk past someone and discern that they have cancer or some other ailment. We start feeling what other people around us are feeling. We may think these are our own social anxieties, but they are theirs. If God reveals it, He wants to heal it. Soul judges soul. Spirit judges spirit. When the disciples wanted to call down fire from heaven on a group of people, Jesus said, **"You do not know what manner of spirit you are of" (see Luke 9:55).** The disciples had a thought, but that thought came from the voice of Satan or demons.

How big is the Holy Spirit in us? As big as our spirit is to contain Him. Pray in the Spirit to build yourself up on your most holy faith (see Jude 1:20). Read the Word daily. Don't just settle for an impartation. When the Holy Spirit grows in you, you'll walk in the Spirit and not fulfill the lust of the flesh (see Galatians 5:16). You'll know all things by the Spirit and all the gifts of the Spirit will be available to be released through you.

> **When He had stopped speaking, He said to Simon, "Launch out into the deep and let down your nets for a catch."**

But Simon answered and said to Him, "Master, we have toiled all night and caught nothing; nevertheless at Your word I will let down the net." And when they had done this, they caught a great number of fish, and their net was breaking. So they signaled to their partners in the other boat to come and help them. And they came and filled both the boats, so that they began to sink. When Simon Peter saw it, he fell down at Jesus' knees, saying, "Depart from me, for I am a sinful man, O Lord!" (Luke 5:4-8).

Jesus instructed them to let down their nets (plural). Peter only let down one net, and that net broke. They should have obeyed Jesus and let down all their nets. Jesus had a bigger supernatural display in mind for them than what their natural minds could think or imagine. They limited the supernatural in their lives by disobeying, listening to their soul, and only letting down one net. Their spiritual capacity to receive did not match the Father's capacity to give, and their nets broke. They were unwilling to enlarge their hearts' capacity to receive.

DISCUSSION QUESTIONS

1. Paul said by "beholding" the glory of the Lord, we are being transformed into Christ's image from glory to glory (see 2 Corinthians 3:18). In your own words, what does it mean to "behold" the glory of the Lord and be transformed into Christ's image? How does this happen? What role does God play and what role do we play in this process?

2. In your own words, what does it mean for Christ's life to be the *only* life in us? (see Galatians 2:20)

3. According to the Bible, what three parts of man must be sanctified? (see 1 Thessalonians 5:23)

4. If man is a tripart being, which part does God speak to? (see Romans 8:16; 1 Corinthians 2:14)

5. What is generally regarded as the biggest hindrance to the Spirit of God speaking to us? Explain.

6. Name some ways both we and God can "break" the human soul.

7. Explain how "breaking" our soul will help us perceive the prophetic?

8. What are some ways we can increase our spirit's capacity to receive from God, especially supernatural things?

9. How will we know when the prophetic is fully activated in our lives? What will that look like?

POSTURING FOR
the Prophetic

Personally, one of the most important disciplines I have found that postures me to receive prophetic revelation is what I call, "The lost art of waiting on the Lord." **"But they that wait upon the Lord shall renew their strength; they shall mount up with wings as eagles; they shall run, and not weary; and they shall walk, and not faint" (Isaiah 40:31, KJV).**

THE LOST ART OF WAITING

Waiting on God became a lost art after Adam sinned. Adam met daily with the Lord and waited.

And they heard the sound of the Lord God walking in the garden in the cool of the day, and Adam and his wife hid themselves from the presence of the Lord God among the trees of the garden.

Then the Lord God called to Adam and said to him, "Where are you?"

So he said, "I heard Your voice in the garden, and I was afraid because I was naked; and I hid myself" (Genesis 3:8-10).

After Adam sinned, God started longing for their routine fellowship. Adam was no longer waiting for Him, so God asked Adam where he was. God was walking in the garden in the cool of the day. He was coming to fellowship with Adam, but when Adam was no longer waiting on the Lord, it broke this routine of sweet, daily fellowship.

> **What is man, that You should exalt him, that You should set Your heart on him, that You should <u>visit him every morning</u>, and test him every moment? (Job 7:17-18)**

> **When I consider Your heavens, the work of Your fingers, the moon and the stars, which You have ordained, what is man that You are mindful of him, and the son of man that <u>You visit him</u>? (Psalm 8:3-4)**

Notice the Lord visits *man*, not just big-name preachers. He desires to visit you. Many people miss out on this great opportunity. God wants to visit us daily, just as He visited Adam before the fall. What happened to Adam, happens to us. God comes looking for us. He wonders, "Why aren't you where you're supposed to be, so we can visit?" Adam was in the garden, the place of visitation. Waiting on God is a life of oneness and union with the Creator. Waiting is a life of coming before Him—knowing, talking, and walking with Him—like the Old Testament saints did. Waiting on God is the key to an intimate relationship with God, to sonship, and to closeness with God.

Waiting on God has also been a lost discipline since the early church, especially after the Eastern and Western Churches split more than a thousand years ago. While the Eastern Orthodox Church retained more of the original concept of waiting on the Lord, the Western Catholic Church was greatly influenced by great thinkers and theologians, and the real definition of "waiting on the Lord" was lost. Even modern Charismatic churches, which operate in spiritual gifts, are not really taught to wait on the Lord. Waiting develops all the inner disciplines—self-control and all the other fruits of the Spirit—and is the doorway to encounters. The Lord once said to me, "My people won't make time to wait on me." This discipline is so important to developing, hearing, and receiving prophetic revelation.

LIKE EAGLES

In Isaiah 40:31, the Lord spoke through the prophet Isaiah using the analogy of eagles. This is called the "like as" principle when Scriptures compare spiritual things to natural things. For example, Psalm 1 compares the man who meditates on God's law day and night to a tree: **"He shall be like a tree planted by the rivers of water" (see Psalm 1:3).**

In Isaiah, the Scripture compares waiting on the Lord to mounting up with wings like eagles. Eagles are also emblematic of the prophetic because eagles have sharp eyes. They have "double vision," meaning they can see things from more than one perspective—at close range and from great distances simultaneously. They can also see downward while looking forward. Their two sets of eyelids also provide amazing peripheral vision. As eagles fly high or even fast, they can spot potential prey on the ground or in the water from miles in the air.

As eagles age, they go through a "molting" or renewal process, which can last for weeks. Their feathers begin to wane and lose strength until they lose their feathers. They become naked and ugly. Their vision also dims. Their claws or talons wear out and become blunt. Calcium deposits build up on their once powerful beaks, making it difficult to tear meat apart or to devour and digest food. Some eagles even die at this stage. However, if they're in good company and surrounded by other eagles, the other eagles will sometimes drop off food for the molting eagles.

Science has confirmed that when eagles reach this stage where they become powerless, they will choose a mountaintop where the eagle can position itself to see the sun unhindered. When it reaches this peak, it will stand with its wings lifted in the air and just stare at the sun without blinking for hours. This will continue for weeks. After weeks of staring at the sun, new feathers begin to grow, new talons emerge, and new beaks develop. For the eagles that endure this molting transformation process, their beauty and youth are restored. The eagle is then totally renewed and changed like a new eagle.

"Who satisfies your mouth with good things, so that your youth is renewed like the eagle's" (Psalm 103:5). To remain a renewed, life-filled eagle, every eagle must endure this molting process until the day it dies. This "like as" is profound. **"They that wait upon the Lord, shall renew their strength, they shall mount up with wings like eagles" (see Isaiah 40:31, KJV).**

Like eagles, every believer can have their spiritual eyes, ears, and senses opened to have "double vision." Every believer can have their feathers renewed and their strength, life, and ability to eat restored, simply by waiting on the Lord.

WHAT IT MEANS TO WAIT ON GOD

"Waiting on God" is like a buried fossil just waiting to be unearthed. Knowing this has become a lost art in the West, Eastern mysticism has claimed and perverted it. Today, many people have only heard of or know the art of waiting from transcendental meditation, yoga, and the New Age movement, which has removed the biblical principles of meditation and separated it from God. People who do not know the history of meditation think it originated with the New Age movement. They don't know the Bible is full of this concept of waiting and meditating on God, which is God's inheritance just waiting to be implemented in our lives.

Waiting can be found nearly 100 times in the Old Testament, 76 times with various shades of meaning, and 21 times in the New Testament with various meanings. Can you think of anything else in the Bible that is mentioned nearly 100 times, yet has been ignored by the church as much as waiting on the Lord? These various usages can be grouped into four categories, giving the term "waiting on the Lord" four general meanings in the Hebrew language.

1. *Raphah*—to be, to stand, or to keep our thoughts and heart activities still. Psalm 46:10 is a great example of this: **"Be still, and know that I am God; I will be exalted among the nations, I will be exalted in the earth!"** It simply means to be still. It does *not* mean to dig in our heals and bolden our resolve.

2. *Dumiyah*—to wait in silence, to remain quiet, to quiet the mind or soul. The mind is hushed or bowed in silence. Psalm 62:1, 5: **"Truly my soul <u>silently waits</u> for God; From Him comes my salvation."** And **"My soul, <u>wait silently</u> for God alone, For my expectation is from Him."**

After I go to the Lord in prayer, speak to the Lord, and pray apostolic prayers, I am still. Think of this like praying through the various stages of the tabernacle. We first come to the brazen altar, which represents sacrifice and repentance in prayer. Then to the washing laver, which represents being washed by the Word. Then we enter the Holy Place, where the seven golden candlesticks are, representing the seven Spirits of God. The light from these lamps enables us to perform our priestly duties, eat from the table of showbread representing Jesus, and go to the altar of incense, which represents praying in the Spirit. Finally, we go beyond the veil to the Holy of Holies and to the ark of the covenant, which represents waiting on the Lord. This leads to encounters. Not coincidentally, just before Samuel received his first prophecy, he was lying near the ark of God, waiting for God to speak (see 1 Samuel 3:3-4).

3. *Qavah*—to be gathered together into oneness, to gather our thoughts and emotions, to remain focused without a single stray thought. Everything within us must wait in oneness. Our thoughts and emotions must be gathered into oneness, and any inner conflict, noise, or brain chatter must be commanded to stop. Genesis 1:9: **"Then God said, 'Let the waters under the heavens be <u>gathered together</u> into one place, and let the dry land appear;' and it was so."** Also, Psalm 25:5: **"Lead me in Your truth and teach me, for You are the God of my salvation; on You I <u>wait</u> all the day."**

4. *Chakah*—to wait earnestly with loving anticipation as a bride waits for her bridegroom. Psalm 33:20: **"Our soul <u>waits</u> for the Lord; He is our help and our shield."** In Song of Solomon 3:1-2, the Shulamite woman waited for her groom: **"By night on my bed I <u>sought</u> the one I love; I <u>sought</u> him, but I did not find him. 'I will rise now,' I said, 'and go about the city; in the streets and in the squares I will <u>seek</u> the one I love.' I <u>sought</u> him, but I did not find him."** At first, we may seek the Lord but not find Him. We may wonder, "What am I doing?" This is so contrary to everything else we do in our fast-paced, busy world, but we keep seeking and waiting for Him *until* we find Him, then we seek and wait for Him again.

In the New Testament, *chakah* was used to describe how the disciples "tarried" or "waited" for the Holy Spirit during the ten days before Pentecost, after which they were endued with power from on high. Some Pentecostals emphasize "tarrying" or waiting, but the 120 were waiting for the Feast of Pentecost and were the only ones in the New Testament who waited. After that initial outpouring, everyone else received the Holy Spirit instantly by exercising their faith. We should tarry for God, but not to receive the Holy Spirit. This is why we often teach people to believe and expect the Holy Spirit to come on them when we pray for them to receive.

Combined, these four definitions summarize waiting on God to mean waiting earnestly in silence and stillness in God's presence, while seeking to be bound in perfect union with the Lord Jesus Christ. As one preacher put it, "After we have prayed verbally, our hearts are intentionally hushed and silenced to hear or see what He might say or show us, to do His bidding."

One of the most difficult things in the world to do is to harness our thoughts. After we have verbally prayed and made our requests known to God, we must subdue our restlessness and resistance to *do*. Then, sit quietly and undistracted in His presence, while harnessing our emotions, senses, thoughts, and imaginations and binding them together in oneness before Him, waiting as long as it takes for our posture to be enough for Him to visit us. When we begin to practice this, sooner or later, the Lord *will* appear to us. And personally, I have received some of my greatest revelations during these times. We must learn to master this art of bringing all that is within us into subjection. God doesn't scream. To hear God, we must silence ourselves and listen over all the other noises that surround us.

COMMUNING WITH THE LORD

Communing with the Lord is the most important thing we can do in this life. Our human tendency is to make it a contribution or a transactional thing. "If I pray long enough, God will reward me." That is not what waiting on the Lord is about. It's not a duty or obligation, it's a relationship. We can get into a lot of trouble by trying to do something *for* God without hearing *from* God. We want Jesus' power and authority to do things without following Jesus' example and practices, like when He left His disciples to go and pray all night. Jesus only did what He saw His Father doing, so He left His disciples to pray all night to see what His Father was doing. Jesus did this because He understood God's voice is often drowned out by the activities and noises around us. Collect your thoughts, put your mind and focus on Him, and give God your undivided attention. Bob Jones always waited on the Lord, then prophesied.

The quieter we are, the more God speaks and does. This develops longsuffering and patience. Moses was on the mountain six days before the Lord spoke to him (see Exodus 24:16). Pray for others, but after you're done praying, master the art of waiting and focusing on Him. We cannot focus on God and be scatterbrained.

> **"I am the vine, you are the branches. He who abides in Me, and I in him, bears much fruit; for without Me you can do nothing ... "If you abide in Me, and My words abide in you, you will ask what you desire, and it shall be done for you"** **(John 15:5, 7).**

The word **"abide"** here in the Greek is *meno*, which means to dwell, continue, stay, or remain. Fruitfulness comes from this practice. The tendency within us is to always *do* more. However, when we enter into this state of waiting, we actually *do* less and rest in His presence. This allows the still small voice of the Lord to be heard (see 1 Kings 19:12). The prophetic words of the Lord are in the atmosphere, just waiting to be heard. Unfortunately, most Christians never posture themselves in the required way to hear or receive what God is saying. Waiting allows us to subdue and take our thoughts captive until His thoughts become ours.

"My soul, wait silently for God alone, for my expectation is from Him" (Psalm 62:5). Waiting silently is counterintuitive to those who think prayer is one-sided; that we do all the talking, then end with an abrupt, "Amen!" This is especially difficult for Pentecostals and Charismatics who feel they need to be praying or singing in tongues the whole time. However, every prophet in the Bible who received a true word from the Lord also received a real visitation from the Lord. Perhaps we haven't waited long enough for a real visitation. As we wait silently, we take captive the brain chatter with the expectation that God will come. We must wait in silence, always expecting the Lord to come. As we take seriously this discipline, we must believe that God desires this in us and desires to appear and visit us.

"There remains therefore a rest for the people of God. For he who has entered His rest has himself also ceased from his works as God did from His" (Hebrews 4:9-10). The truth is, the more we rest, the more God works. Think about it. On Adam's first full day, there was rest and communion with God. God visited with man. This is also a beautiful picture of our spiritual state with God in the new covenant. The seventh day sabbath is yet another spiritual picture for new covenant believers. When we cease from all physical and mental activities to visit with the Lord, God visits us just like Adam.

"For since the beginning of the world men have not heard nor perceived by the ear, nor has the eye seen any God besides You, Who acts for the one who waits for Him" (Isaiah 64:4). Now compare this to 1 Corinthians 2:9: **"But as it is written, 'Eye has not seen, nor ear heard, nor have entered into the heart of man the things which God has prepared for those who love Him.'"**

LOVING THE LORD

1 Corinthians 2:9 is quoted from Isaiah 64:4. Paul often quoted Old Testament Scriptures in his New Testament Epistles to shed light on the actual meaning and fulfillment of those

verses. Notice Isaiah said, **"for the one who *waits* for Him,"** while Paul said, **"for those who *love* Him."** New Testament love is equated with Old Testament waiting. Waiting for Him and loving Him is the same, like a lover waits for her bridegroom. Waiting is based on love. Waiting and loving are like a double-edged sword. We're not fully sharp if we have one without the other. The Lord receives our love for Him in the form of waiting. Waiting on the Lord is God's love language. When we understand that waiting on the Lord is God's love language, we will do this in fulfillment of the great commandment. Things perceived that the eye and ear cannot perceive are received by those who love *and* wait for Him.

"He who has My commandments and keeps them, it is he who loves Me. And he who loves Me will be loved by My Father, and I will love him <u>and manifest Myself to him</u>" (John 14:21). If you want a visitation from the Lord, this is your verse. Obey His commandments and love the Son, and the Father and Jesus will love you and Jesus will manifest Himself to you. Jesus wants to reveal Himself to us, and waiting is key to making this a reality. To have a visitation, we must first be invited, and the Lord invites us. He wants to visit us and make Himself real to us.

> **Jesus said to him, "You shall love the Lord your God with all your heart, with all your soul, and with all your mind.' This is the first and greatest commandment. And the second is like it: 'You shall love your neighbor as yourself.' On these two commandments hang all the Law and the Prophets"** (Matthew 22:37-40).

Waiting on the Lord is one major way to show our love for God. When we gather all our thoughts and emotions in one place and focus on Him without allowing our minds to wander, we'll understand that loving the Lord with all our heart, soul, mind, and strength means waiting on Him. I truly have found this discipline to be the most important form for posturing myself to receive visitations and revelations from Almighty God. So, now that you know this, what are you "waiting" for? Waiting on God doesn't require us to do much, yet it requires us to do everything.

AN END-TIME REMNANT WHO WAIT

The Lord has shown me that, before the great end-time outpouring, there will be a remnant of believers in the church who will wait on Him in communion, like the Old Testament saints. If we are under **"a better covenant ... established on better promises" (see Hebrews 8:6)**, our experiences should be better than theirs. The further we go back in the Old Testament, the more we find real communion with God—Adam, Enoch, Noah, Abraham, and Moses—but by the time we reach the end of the Old Testament there's complete silence—no open visions or visitations by God. Theologians say there was also a 400-year period of prophetic silence between Malachi, the last prophet in the Old Testament, and John the Baptist, the first prophet in the New Testament.

The more sin became embedded in the psyche and DNA of man, the more the fellowship between God and man became fragmented. Jesus, the last Adam, became the doorway to restore this relationship, so man could once again **"come boldly to the throne of grace"** to **"obtain mercy and find grace to help in time of need" (see Hebrews 4:16)**. This is more than just theology and requires more than just head knowledge. Moses came face-to-face with the Lord on the mountain for seven days, but we have a better covenant. Therefore, we should expect more, not less.

I understand that not everyone has been gifted to see angels. I'm talking about a lifestyle of seeing and communing with God that exists outside any gift. This is for everyone. Just because certain religious traditions say there is no active communion with God doesn't mean you and I cannot have communion with God. This is not a gift. Communion with God is a benefit of sonship, of becoming sons and daughters of God through salvation. This is also nearness to God (see Hebrews 10:22; James 4:8). We will soon see a large number of Christians having experiences with the Lord like the Old Testament saints did. This will take place just before the end-time outpouring and will supersede anything seen by the Old Testament saints.

All our modern distractions, like cell phones and social media, have interfered with our waiting on God. We have little control over what we process in the deep recesses of our thinking because whatever we expose ourselves to gets stuck there. Repentance is a choice, and we must choose willpower. Waiting on God helps us develop the fruit of the Spirit. Patience is one of them, though it's the least desired fruit. Waiting is a lost art, just as "patience" or "longsuffering" is a lost fruit. This fruit is not talked about nearly as much as the others. Yet, patiently waiting on God is the most significant doorway to encountering God *and* the supernatural. This is where the Lord visits us. Some time ago, the Lord said to me, "My people don't make time to wait on Me, and that is why they miss out on encounters that bring revelation." Do we make time?

DISCUSSION QUESTIONS

1. Why do you think "waiting on the Lord" has become a lost art, a lost discipline, or even a lost fruit?

2. According to Psalm 8:4, the Lord visits man. According to Job 7:18, the Lord visits man every morning. With that in mind, why do you think the Lord doesn't visit more people? Explain.

3. Isaiah 40:31 compares waiting on the Lord to mounting up with wings like eagles. In what other ways could "waiting on the Lord" be compared to eagles?

4. Psalm 103:5 says that God will renew our youth like the eagles. What does this mean?

5. What are the meanings of the four Hebrew words translated "wait" in the Old Testament?

6. Based on these four definitions, how would you define "waiting on the Lord" in your own words?

7. Why is "communing with the Lord" the most important thing we can do in this life?

8. Explain how "waiting on the Lord" and "loving the Lord" are the same? (see Isaiah 64:4; 1 Corinthians 2:9)

9. If there is an end-time remnant of believers in the church who will wait on the Lord in communion with Him, do you feel you will be a part of this remnant? Why or why not?

"Like eagles, every believer can have their spiritual eyes, ears, and senses opened to have 'double vision.'"

PATIENCE WITH
the Prophetic

"For all the promises of God in Him are Yes, and in Him Amen, to the glory of God through us" (2 Corinthians 1:20). God is faithful. His promises to us are totally reliable, yet steps are often required while contending for these prophetic promises until they come to pass or until they can be applied to our lives. Here are a few:

1. Accept and agree with what God has said He will do.

2. Stay in faith and patience so the fulfillment of the promise will remain possible.

3. Take the necessary steps to show you truly believe the prophetic word that was spoken.

FAITH OR PRESUMPTION?

Abraham and Sarah were given the seemingly impossible promise that they would have a son in their old age. This promise was sovereign but not without human responsibility and alignment. Abraham and Sarah could have stepped out of alignment or stopped having intimate relations with one another, and the promise would not have come, since there was only one virgin birth. However, Abraham and Sarah also took inappropriate steps by trying to self-fulfill the prophecy through

Sarah's handmaid, Hagar. Hagar and Abraham then gave birth to a son whose descendants would end up fighting against the family of promise for thousands of years.

When God makes a sovereign promise, we still need to practice wisdom and balance. We do this by keeping ourselves aligned with what God said, and by not trying to initiate the outcome of the promise ourselves. Trying to self-fulfill a prophecy may seem innocent at first but can have drastic consequences.

Abraham and Sarah likely felt they were demonstrating faith in God's promise by trying to help make it come true, when in actuality it was an act of presumption. Presumption can be defined as arrogant behavior that transgresses the limits of what is appropriate or to act with brash or brazen audacity. It is the arrogance of excessive self-confidence. In short, presumption is an action not wholly in line with the nature and character of God.

Abraham's sexual relations with Hagar may have been culturally acceptable at the time, but the heart of God is for monogamy, which is an intimate covenant between one man and one woman. Our response to a prophetic word should never draw us away from godly behavior, which is the fruit of the Spirit. What we do in response to a prophetic word should look like what Jesus would do.

FAITH AND PATIENCE

Still, we should not be so afraid of being presumptuous that we fail to take the appropriate steps of faith. King Saul's son, Jonathan, once attacked an enemy outpost without a direct command from God and without his father's knowledge. How was that not presumption? Yet, Jonathan based the entire attack on who God had shown Himself to be. Jonathan said to his armor-bearer, **"Come, let us go over to the garrison of these uncircumcised; it may be that the Lord will work for us. For nothing restrains the Lord from saving by many or by few"** (see 1 Samuel 14:6). It always goes back to this whole idea of waiting on the Lord.

> **By your steadfastness and <u>patient endurance</u> you shall win the true life of your souls (Luke 21:19 AMP).**

> **And we desire that each one of you show the same diligence to the full assurance of hope until the end, that you do not become sluggish, but imitate those who through <u>faith and patience</u> inherit the promises (Hebrews 6:11-12).**

There's just something about impatience that causes us to pay dearly. We want things when we want them, but God is eternal and not constrained by time. We must trust Him through the process of developing revelation and never try to force or rush something. We must always recognize it is okay to receive parts of a prophecy until time progresses and the picture fully develops. This enables us to develop the fruit of the Spirit and teaches us the value and importance of longsuffering and waiting on the Lord to receive clarity. Impatience always leads to the worst, most drastic decisions. I have learned that a decision made in reaction to another decision made usually turns out to be the wrong decision.

JESUS HEALS A LAME MAN

After this there was a feast of the Jews, and Jesus went up to Jerusalem. Now there is in Jerusalem by the Sheep Gate a pool, which is called in Hebrew, Bethesda, having five porches. In these lay a great multitude of sick people, blind, lame, paralyzed, waiting for the moving of the water. For an angel went down at a certain time into the pool and stirred up the water; then whoever stepped in first, after the stirring

of the water, was made well of whatever disease he had. Now a certain man was there who had an infirmity thirty-eight years. When Jesus saw him lying there, and knew that he already had been in that condition a long time, He said to him, "Do you want to be made well?"

The sick man answered Him, "Sir, I have no man to put me into the pool when the water is stirred up; but while I am coming, another steps down before me."

Jesus said to him, "Rise, take up your bed and walk." And immediately the man was made well, took up his bed, and walked.

And that day was the Sabbath. The Jews therefore said to him who was cured, "It is the Sabbath; it is not lawful for you to carry your bed." He answered them, "He who made me well said to me, 'Take up your bed and walk.'"

Then they asked him, "Who is the Man who said to you, 'Take up your bed and walk'?" But the one who was healed did not know who it was, for Jesus had withdrawn, a multitude being in that place. Afterward Jesus found him in the temple, and said to him, "See, you have been made well." Sin no more, lest a worse thing come upon you."

The man departed and told the Jews that it was Jesus who had made him well (John 5:1-15).

Any time people are more concerned about rules than getting people healed, or more concerned about a religious system than the supernatural activity of God, that is a religious spirit. Here in John 5, we see one of eight signs Jesus performed in His early ministry to show He was the Messiah. Turning water into wine was the first, but each had significant meaning. The pool of Bethesda had five porches, and five is the number of grace. *Bethesda* also means kindness, so whoever had the drive or initiative to jump in first, could plunge into the depths of God's kindness and grace to receive whatever they needed to be made whole.

BREAKING MINDSETS

To be "made whole" or "made well" doesn't just mean getting our problems fixed; it also means breaking the mindsets and thinking patterns that keep us sick, defeated, discouraged, and downtrodden. God is more interested in breaking our thinking patterns than He is in fixing any particular situation we are in, because when those thinking patterns are broken, all the other problems can be fixed. Some problems can actually be symptoms of our thinking patterns.

In Bethesda, these five porches were filled with people with all kinds of ailments and problems, yet Jesus only spoke to one man. Some were blind; others were paralyzed or lame. No doubt other unmentioned infirmities were represented, but all were waiting for that moment, that "suddenly from God" when an angel came down to stir the water. Of course, some people debate whether this was a legend or really true. Nevertheless, the Bible says, **"an angel went down at a certain time,"** and I tend to believe the Bible.

Which porch they were on may have depended on their condition, but what brought them all together was they each had something wrong with them that disrupted their lives. They were stuck in the holding pattern of people who were not yet dead but also not living. We also can be dead inside while still living. This particular man Jesus spoke to had been in this holding pattern for thirty-eight years.

Maybe you're also in a holding pattern, waiting for a divine moment or a divine intervention from God to fix whatever has kept you paralyzed, inactive, disengaged, or unable to live a normal, healthy life and fulfill your purpose in society. These people were not in the cemetery yet, but neither were they experiencing abundant life. Still, every day, they took pride in the fact they had survived. Many people today are in this same place spiritually, mentally, and emotionally.

The pathological mindset that revolved around this pool was, "I should not expect more. I'm just going to adopt the mentality of my environment and be content with making the best of a bad situation rather than expect change." We see this exact mindset when Jesus asked this man, "Do you want to be made whole?" Notice he did not say, "Yes, please!" Instead, he said, "I have no one to help me in the pool. Someone else always steps in first." He had tunnel vision, thinking God could only work one way. We, too, can have tunnel vision regarding the ways ministry can happen or the ways God can move or change our situations. We get stuck in our minds and paralyzed by our own mentalities more than our physical ailments.

THE ABUNDANT LIFE

Jesus said, **"I have come that they might have life, and that they may have it more abundantly" (see John 10:10).** However, the sick man had been waiting in this state for thirty-eight years. He was not living a happy life. Instead of bringing his expectation level up to Jesus' reality, he brought his expectation level down to his reality. He lowered his expectations about what God could do to avoid perpetual disappointment. He didn't know the One who asked him the question could do **"exceedingly abundantly above all that we ask or think" (see Ephesians 3:20).**

If God can do bigger and better, why do we let our environment lower our expectations, causing us perpetual physical, mental, emotional, and spiritual paralyses? Again, this man had been in this state for thirty-eight years, surrounded by other people with similar problems who said, "At least they didn't carry me off to the morgue today." Following His Father's lead, Jesus intentionally went to that one man that day, knowing God wanted to disrupt this man's thinking. "You're not going to the morgue today; you're going to take up your bed and walk today! Don't get stuck in a rut thinking God can only heal you one way." Jesus' response to his inability to get in the pool was, **"Rise, take up your bed and walk."**

Jesus is asking us the same question: "Do you want to be made whole, or are you comfortable and complacent with being broken?" Are you expecting more, or are you experiencing tunnel vision? If you're down and discouraged and everyone else around you is down and discouraged, that becomes normal. The enemy wants to keep you focused on your situation.

The only common ground we have with some people is complaining. Don't become bedfellows with people who don't think higher than you. Find people who will demand the best of you and not cater to your complacent mentality. I've heard people complain that preaching goes over their head; they'd rather hear something simpler. Sometimes we need preaching and teaching that goes over our heads to call us up to a higher level of understanding and expectation.

We also need to prophesy and **"call those things which do not exist as though they did" (see Romans 4:17).** We need to see the gold in the dirt and the possibilities in the impossibilities. And we all need people in our lives to tell us what God sees in us that we *don't* see. God doesn't speak or prophesy to where we are. He calls us "the father of many nations" before we even have a child. He speaks to our potential. I've known good speakers, singers, writers, and many gifted and anointed people who could not escape the culture of dysfunction around them, so they just remained on their dysfunctional porches. Many people never make their lives better or expect more of themselves. We all need sympathy and compassion, but we also need people who will challenge our thinking and not let us remain on our dysfunctional porches.

A lion is "king of the jungle." He roars, he roams, he has claws and teeth, he eats and devours. But if you take that lion out of the jungle and put him in a zoo or in a cage with walls, it takes the life right out of him. His behavior changes, he loses his prowess, he just lies around and sleeps. He's no longer a lion but a contradiction to his identity. He's a lying lion.

Some people spend years in prison until the fight dies out of them and prison becomes their new norm, but Jesus said, **Therefore if the Son makes you free, you shall be free indeed"** **(John 8:36).** Jesus did not *set* us free; He *made* us free. If we're *set* free, we can be bound again, but when we're *made* free, we can never be bound again. When we're *made* free, we're free to be who God made us to be.

WE BECOME WHO WE HANG AROUND

If you want to know what "porch" you're on, just look at your cell phone address book or Facebook friends list. That will tell you what porch you're on. Who do you spend your time talking to? If you're blind, you'll be on the blind porch, and the only reason you're on the blind porch is because you found other people there who could sympathize with your blindness because they were also blind. We all need people who understand us, but we also need prophetic people who will declare war on our blindness. So long as we hang around blind people, we'll never have faith to see.

We cannot hang out with angry people and expect to be happy. We cannot hang out with complainers and expect to be full of faith. I like what Bill Johnson says, "If God inhabits the praises of His people, who inhabits the complaints?" We can invite God or the devil into our lives simply by the attitudes of our hearts and the words that come from our mouths. Jesus said it's **"what comes out of man, that defiles a man" (see Mark 7:20).**

If you want to invite God in your life and God inhabits praise, start praising the people in your work environment. Praise them for the quality of their work and for the job they do. If you want to invite God in your home, start praising your family members. If you want to invite God in your church, start praising one another. Wherever you want to invite God, bring praise because God inhabits it. We can invite God into any situation this way.

We cannot hang out with defeated, discouraged, downtrodden people and expect to be overcomers. If we're not being salt and light, encouraging the discouraged, then we become like them. If we're not speaking faith and calling those things which do not exist as though they did, then we will become discouraged.

Jesus spoke peace to the storm when everyone else was bailing water. **"Teacher, do You not care that we are perishing?" (see Mark 4:38)** They woke Him up. How could He sleep through a storm? How could He speak peace to a storm? **"Peace, be still!" (see Mark 4:39).** Because He had internal peace, there was no storm inside Him. If we're full of internal, emotional, and spiritual storms, we cannot speak to external storms. What gives us authority to speak to those storms is having joy and peace within. In the midst of affliction, we can have peace, even when we don't understand what's happening.

We become who we hang around. You'll never soar with the eagles while nesting with the chickens. Birds of a feather flock together, and so do destinies. What porch are you on? We cannot hang out with arrogant people and be humble. Sometimes we connect with people who share the same problems, but this only enables and empowers us and them to remain unchanged.

These people on these five porches literally built a system and infrastructure based on survival. How many times have we based our mental structures and thinking patterns on what we feel we cannot change? We think we cannot fix it, so we just add air-conditioning and padded seats. "If I'm going to remain paralyzed, I might as well build a comfortable bed to sleep on." After thirty-eight years, this man had lost faith that his condition could ever change and surrounded himself with people who enabled him to remain unchanged. Then he started blaming others: "No one helps me get in the water. Someone always steps in before me."

DO YOU WANT TO BE MADE WELL?

Jesus is the answer to all our problems, but that day the Answer asked a question. The Bible says, **"When Jesus saw him lying there, and knew that he already had been in that condition a long time, He said to him, 'Do you want to be made well?'"** I used to think that was a silly question, but it isn't silly because so many people get comfortable with their problems. In fact, they're not happy unless something's wrong. Their whole lives and identities are built around their problems. Jesus asked this question because He saw he had been there for a long time. Nothing in this man's actions indicated he wanted to be healed. If he did get well, he might have an identity crisis. He might have to become a missionary or a prophetic voice. He might have to start a ministry, or rescue people from human trafficking, or change the world.

Some people have a hard time seeing themselves well or actually doing what God has placed in their heart to do, like being a schoolteacher, business owner, author, politician, agent of change, or world changer. Without their handicap, they don't know who they are. They'd rather just lie back down. This is why on the night God delivered the Israelites from Egypt and while they ate the Passover Lamb, He said, **"And thus you shall eat it: with a belt on your waist, your sandals on your feet, and your staff in your hand" (see Exodus 12:11).** God was getting ready to make a change in their lives, so they needed to be ready and expecting deliverance.

If all this man wanted to do was survive, then Jesus asked him a legitimate question: **"Do you want to be made well?"** God will do nothing against our wills. We must be in total faith and agreement with God's will, not only with our words but also with our actions. Our response will tell whether we're in agreement with God's purposes. Some people self-sabotage their success by running away from those who love them, just when things start getting better. They'll find one bad thing to focus on and mess everything else up. They have an addiction to affliction. Before we can change, we must first repent. The Greek word repent is *metanoeo*, which means "to change one's mind." To change our lives, we must first change our minds.

This man did not answer Jesus' question. All he said was it wasn't his fault he wasn't healed. He had no help, support, or opportunity. People blame their problems on their parents, their skin color, or how they were raised to justify their condition and remain the same. Someone always beat him to the water. Sometimes we have to want something bad enough to beat others to it. Sometimes we have to be willing to press through the crowd, like the woman who touched the hem of Jesus' garment. *Bethesda* means "kindness," and five means grace. These people were so close to their breakthrough and diving into God's grace and kindness.

We look for others to help us, motivate us, or encourage us to take a big step like going to school, joining a church, or starting a ministry. We wait for others to push us in when God is waiting on us to dive into His grace and kindness. He loves us like crazy, and He doesn't want us to remain the same. It's time to jump in, take the plunge, and quit tiptoeing around with our "barely-get-by" mentalities. The pessimistic Christian says, "the cup is half empty." The optimistic Christian says, "the cup is half full." The overcoming Christian says, **"My cup runs over" (see Psalm 23:5).**

Jesus told this man to take his bed as evidence of his life change and of the life-changing power of God. The bed became his testimony. Everyone who saw him carry that bed remembered who he once was and who he now was, after he encountered the Master and was made whole. Through faith *and* patience, we inherit the promises.

I'd like to leave you with this blessing: "In the name of the Lord Jesus Christ, I break the power of delay off your life. It's time to step into the deep. Come on in, the water's fine. Rise, take up your bed and walk!"

DISCUSSION QUESTIONS

1. What role does faith play in seeing prophetic words come to pass or applying them to our lives? Explain.

2. What role does patience play in seeing prophetic words come to pass and applying them to our lives? Explain.

3. In your own words, define presumption. How does presumption differ from faith?

4. What stands out to you most about the story of Jesus healing the lame man at the pool of Bethesda? Why?

5. Why is breaking mindsets so important to receiving prophetic healing and deliverance? Explain.

6. Instead of the lame man bringing his expectation level up to Jesus' reality, he brought his expectation level down to his reality. Explain the role of faith in living the abundant life Jesus spoke of in John 10:10.

7. In addition to our hearts' attitudes and words coming out of our mouths, who we hang around is important. Why?

8. Why was Jesus' question to the lame man, "Do you want to be made well?" *not* a silly question?

9. Do you have a hard time seeing your life or circumstances changing for the better? What if Jesus were to ask you today, "Do you want to be made well?" What would be your answer and why?

"Prophetic words of warning enable the church to know how to pray, intercede, respond, and prepare."

PRACTICING
the Prophetic

So He came to a city of Samaria which is called Sychar, near the plot of ground that Jacob gave to his son Joseph. Now Jacob's well was there. Jesus therefore, being wearied from His journey, sat thus by the well. It was about the sixth hour.

A woman of Samaria came to draw water. Jesus said to her, "Give Me a drink." For His disciples had gone away into the city to buy food.

Then the woman of Samaria said to Him, "How is it that You, being a Jew, ask a drink from me, a Samaritan woman?" For Jews have no dealings with Samaritans.

Jesus answered and said to her, "If you knew the gift of God, and who it is who says to you, 'Give Me a drink,' you would have asked Him, and He would have given you living water."

The woman said to Him, "Sir, You have nothing to draw with, and the well is deep. Where then do You get that living water? Are You greater than our father Jacob, who gave us the well, and drank from it himself, as well as his sons and his livestock?"

Jesus answered and said to her, "Whoever drinks of this water will thirst again, but whoever drinks of the water that

I shall give him will never thirst. But the water that I shall give him will become in him a fountain of water springing up into everlasting life."

The woman said to Him, "Sir, give me this water, that I may not thirst, nor come here to draw."

Jesus said to her, "Go, call your husband, and come here."

The woman answered and said, "I have no husband."

Jesus said to her, "You have well said, 'I have no husband,' for you have had five husbands, and the one whom you now have is not your husband; in that you spoke truly."

The woman said to Him, "Sir, I perceive that You are a prophet. Our fathers worshiped on this mountain, and you Jews say that in Jerusalem is the place where one ought to worship."

Jesus said to her, "Woman, believe Me, the hour is coming when you will neither on this mountain, nor in Jerusalem, worship the Father. You worship what you do not know; we know what we worship, for salvation is of the Jews. But the hour is coming, and now is, when the true worshipers will worship the Father in spirit and truth; for the Father is seeking such to worship Him. God is Spirit, and those who worship Him must worship in spirit and truth."

The woman said to Him, "I know that Messiah is coming" (who is called Christ). "When He comes, He will tell us all things."

Jesus said to her, "I who speak to you am He.
And at this point His disciples came, and they marveled that He talked with a woman; yet no one said, "What do You seek?" or, "Why are You talking with her?"

The woman then left her waterpot, went her way into the city, and said to the men, "Come, see a Man who told me all things that I ever did. Could this be the Christ?" Then they went out of the city and came to Him (John 4:5-30).

PROPHETIC LESSONS FROM JESUS

This Samaritan woman discovered the purpose of prophecy—to heal people and make them whole. Not only did Jesus not pass judgment on her, He also showed that He could cross social, religious, cultural, geographical, gender, and every other boundary with the prophetic. He took the risk of having her reject what He said to her. Not every prophetic story ends positively when we step out and prophesy. Some people will reject you or try to make you feel stupid. This woman carried so much shame she tried to cover it. She had built up walls, hardened herself, and didn't want to make herself vulnerable.

When many people read this story, they see a delicate scenario. What do we do when we feel God is giving us a prophetic word that will call out sin? If we don't have authority or have not been given permission to speak into someone's life, it is not our place to prophesy because they can be further hardened and feel even more shame.

In our current society, we can no longer speak with a common moral framework. Once upon a time, a man and woman living together outside of marriage was considered morally inappropriate, but today we cannot speak to this without being judged. In fact, America's current culture doesn't even allow us to speak constructive words of correction, unless we first build trust. We must win hearts before we can win beliefs. We must not only teach and preach the good news, but we must also model what it looks like to be a contributing member of society.

We need to be careful when we prophesy to people and not use prophecy to correct people's lives. That's why we have the Word of God. Also, be careful not to **"cast your pearls before swine, lest they trample them under their feet, and turn and tear you to pieces" (see Matthew 7:6).** Prophetic words are for building people up, not tearing them down. Know when and when not to use the prophetic gift. The Samaritan woman understood correctly that prophetic words brought healing and wholeness to her life.

Jesus also left the "race card" out of the conversation. He did not address the Jews vs. Samaritans debate. She pointed out what separated them; Jesus looked for common ground. The Jews in Galilee and Judea in Jesus' day shunned Samaritans because they viewed them as a mixed race who practiced an impure, half-pagan religion.

Jesus gave her a chance to be vulnerable. When people carry shame, they must become vulnerable for them to be cured. Jesus gave her a chance to talk about her broken marriages and demonstrated a continued interest in her. He even went out of His way to go to this well to meet her. No doubt He heard from the Father and went there just for her. Her response showed the opposite of shame. And, by asking for a drink, Jesus demonstrated that He valued her, though she was a Samaritan and not a Jew.

We must see people through our Father's eyes to be entrusted with prophetic words for them. If we do, they will begin to trust us. The Father first wants to see that we have matured with His heart and eyes for people. We must create atmospheres and environments in which people feel safe. Otherwise, we will only preach superficially without penetrating hearts. God is looking for people who are imperfect but also real and authentic. To **"worship the Father in spirit and truth,"** as in John 4:24, means to be genuine, real, authentic, and transparent. To preach and stand for truth also means to be genuine and transparent.

Vulnerability breeds authenticity. Forget how others want you to be. Be vulnerable toward others, and others will be authentic toward you. Every Christian has been hurt. Be transparent. A religious spirit will cause us to erect walls and false pretenses. It's healthier to keep trying than to give up and refuse to engage others.

Because Jesus demonstrated the Father's heart for this woman, though she was in sin, she was healed relationally. She believed in the prophetic, and this sparked a revival when she arrived back in town. She said, **"Come, see a Man who told me all things that I ever did. Could this be the Christ?"** The town's people went out to see Him. Prophecy built a bridge over seemingly irreparable divisions. When you hear the Father's heart for people, you will love and connect with people who are in sin.

Our prayer should be, "Father, give us Your heart and Your eyes." Prophecy always speaks to the potential in people, even when they themselves don't see it. Still, there are New Testament examples of prophecies that involved corrective warnings, though some in the church today do not believe corrective warnings have a place in New Testament prophecy.

LESSONS FOR PERSONAL PROPHECIES

On the next day we who were Paul's companions departed and came to Caesarea, and entered the house of Philip the evangelist, who was one of the seven, and stayed with him. Now this man had four virgin daughters who prophesied. And as we stayed many days, a certain prophet named Agabus came down from Judea. When he had come to us, he took Paul's belt, bound his own hands and feet,

and said, "Thus says the Holy Spirit, 'so shall the Jews at Jerusalem bind the man who owns this belt, and deliver him into the hands of the Gentiles'"

Now when we heard these things, both we and those from that place pleaded with him not to go up to Jerusalem. Then Paul answered, "What do you mean by weeping and breaking my heart? For I am ready not only to be bound, but also to die at Jerusalem for the name of the Lord Jesus."

So when he would not be persuaded, we ceased, saying, "The will of the Lord be done" (Acts 21:8-14).

Here, after the prophet Agabus had given a prophetic word about a worldwide famine, he now gives a personal prophecy to Paul. It takes a special grace to do both. Personally, I have noticed whenever I am in a season of anointing for international prophecies, personal prophecies take a back seat.

How this prophecy to Paul was interpreted gives us some principles for interpreting personal prophecies: how Paul received it, how it was given, and how others interpreted it. Paul was already on his way to Jerusalem. In Acts 19:21, **"Paul purposed in the Spirit"** or felt compelled by the Spirit to go to Jerusalem, and then to Rome. In Acts 20:16, **"he was hurrying to be at Jerusalem, if possible, on the Day of Pentecost."** It seemed Agabus' word contradicted Paul's word, or did it?

In Agabus' previous prophecy regarding worldwide famine, Paul had confidence in Agabus' accuracy. He and Barnabas helped send relief to the churches in Judea. Now, led by the Spirit, Agabus gave Paul a personal prophecy. Paul did not ask him for the prophecy. Sometimes people will ask for prophetic words when they are unsure about something.

Agabus was demonstrative. He took Paul's belt, bound it around himself, then gave the prophecy. Agabus did not interpret the prophecy or add to it. Sometimes people will ask us to tell them more. Just be the mailman and deliver the message. God will trust us with more when we handle His words correctly. Agabus delivered the word verbatim, as he received it, then stopped. Prophets are not psychics. We do not get paid by the hour. When a church starts living from one prophetic word to the next instead of being led by the Holy Spirit, God will pull back on the prophetic in that church.

There were four parts to Agabus' prophecy: 1) Jerusalem, 2) the Jews, 3) Paul would be bound, 4) then handed over to the Jews. This showed that God trusted Agabus. He could trust him enough to give negative words and not just words of affirmation. At the same time, Agabus' prophetic words showed that prophecies *can* be negative words and not just affirmations.

The prophecy said something terrible would happen to Paul in Jerusalem. We should not desire to say anything that God does not absolutely give us. Sometimes hurt people will prophesy doom and gloom out of hurt or anger. However, our eschatology can also affect our prophecies. Sometimes people will prophesy doom and gloom because those are their end-time beliefs.

Don't reject a prophecy just because it's not uplifting or doesn't say something good. Notice Paul did not reject Agabus' prophecy. Also, notice Agabus did not give Paul any specific directions. He only said what would happen. He did not prescribe any action; he simply gave a word. Agabus demonstrated the word but did not use hype to add to it. In fact, he remained neutral about whether Paul should go and only spoke once. He did not use hype or manipulation to benefit himself, his following, or how others saw him. He had no "bone" in the fight.

Then, Paul's companions and those who were at Philip's house urged Paul not to go to Jerusalem. Don't let other people's opinions define or interpret a word for you. They all loved Paul and were concerned about his safety. He was heading for mortal danger, so they urged him not to go. Their well-intentioned words were not based on what God told Agabus nor on what God told Paul.

They interpreted the word from a purely sincere, human viewpoint. They interpreted the word as a word *not* to go to Jerusalem, which was logical. They viewed it as a warning. For Paul, however, it was only more confirmation to go. Agabus was hearing right, and Paul was hearing right. Everyone else's opinions just muddied the waters. They had "confirmation bias," which is the tendency to seek only words that confirm our own personal thoughts and beliefs.

Paul was adamant: **"What do you mean by weeping and breaking my heart? For I am ready not only to be bound, but also to die in Jerusalem for the name of the Lord Jesus" (see Acts 21:13).** Remember when Peter warned Jesus not to go to Jerusalem? Jesus said, **"Get behind Me, Satan!" (see Matthew 16:23).** He wasn't calling Peter Satan, but the spirit *behind* Peter's words. Since Paul could not be otherwise persuaded, they ceased and concluded, **"The will of the Lord be done."**

Why did Paul reject the interpretation of those who loved him? Why did Paul feel such a strong conviction to go to Jerusalem despite the warning of impending danger? Paul had a personal relationship with the Lord and knew how to hear from the Lord for himself. He did not need to rely on others' words. For him, they were simply confirmations. Agabus' prophecy simply confirmed what God had already told him.

Long before Agabus' warning, the Spirit of God had directly and personally spoken to Paul about going to Jerusalem. Paul interpreted Agabus' word based on the *rhema* word he had already received. When we are following God, true prophecy will simply confirm what we already know. If we're *not* in the Spirit or walking closely with the Lord, prophecy can change our course or direction. We need to ask the Lord to help us by only giving prophetic warnings when they are from Him, rather than from our own suspicions. Sadly, it is quite common when we learn something about someone's life, to give them advice and then incorrectly say, "God told me to tell you."

Many people today disregard prophetic words because they perceive them not as "positive." This prophetic word simply revealed to Paul what would happen to him. Yet many today would reject such a word because it doesn't fit their definition of New Testament prophecy, nor is it something they want to hear. "Confirmation bias" is one of the most common reasons for people rejecting personal prophecies. This is an important subject that must be addressed in prophetic ministry.

"Confirmation bias" is when we take new facts or new information and process them only through the lens or narrative of what we believe. So, if information we receive confirms what is already in our hearts, we receive that prophetic word as valid. However, when new information or a prophetic revelation seems to contradict our goals or direction, we immediately reject them because we only hear or accept what confirms what we already believe.

LESSONS FOR INTERNATIONAL PROPHECIES

And in these days prophets came from Jerusalem to Antioch. Then one of them, named Agabus, stood up and showed by the Spirit that there was going to be a great famine throughout all the world, which also happened in the days of Claudius Caesar. Then the disciples, each according to his ability, determined to send relief to the brethren dwelling in Judea. This they also did, and sent it to

the elders by the hands of Barnabas and Saul (Acts 11:27-30).

Here, Agabus prophesied a worldwide famine, which also came to pass. This is a New Testament prophetic word in which God brought judgment. The value of this international prophetic word of warning allowed the church, as a watchman ministry, to begin preparing to send disaster relief to those who would suffer from the famine. This positioned the church to respond to a cultural and societal crisis before it happened. Joseph's interpretation of Pharoah's dream in the Old Testament did the same (see Genesis 41). Because Joseph accurately interpreted Pharoah's dream, Egypt was able to store up food for seven years and brace for the coming famine. They were even able to open up their storehouses to all other nations.

This is why we should never allow a spirit of fear to grip us regarding words of correction, warning, or preparation. Many people confuse preparedness with fear. Preparation is *not* fear. Prophetic words of correction and warning enable the church to know how to pray, intercede, respond, and prepare when trusted prophetic voices speak about a coming national or international crisis. It also empowers the church to help others when trusted prophetic voices speak about what is coming on the world before it comes. This was true in the Old Testament and New Testament, and it remains true today.

After Agabus predicted worldwide famine, he stopped. He did not reference sin. He only spoke about what the Holy Spirit had given him. He did not add his own personal bias to it. Others responded to what he said and collected offerings. We don't know *why* the famine came, but we don't need to know. Over time, I have learned that we don't need to understand all the "whys." Agabus simply said a famine was coming. We know in part and prophesy in part. We get in trouble when we try to prophesy the whole when we only know in part.

When I received the prophecy about Hurricane Ian, we were able to pray and train more than a hundred people at MorningStar to go and help. Similarly, we need to do warfare with the prophecies spoken over our families and children and do what we can to help them, just like when the church responded to Agabus' words.

The famine was negative, and Paul being bound was negative. Much of what we call "prophecy" today is more exhortation and encouragement than prophecy because that is what receives the most social media clicks and views. The prophetic is not about telling people what they want to hear.

In 2020, I cautioned people about QAnon and the conspiracy theories surrounding the 2020 U.S. presidential election. I knew something wasn't right about the 2020 election, but we must be careful not to say more than what God says. God is interested in much more than American politics. Jesus is not an American. God so loved the *world*.

The false prophets in Jeremiah's day said, **"You shall have peace"** and **"No evil shall come upon you" (see Jeremiah 23:17).** The Lord said these false prophets **"prophesy lies. Indeed they are prophets of the deceit of their own hearts" (see Jeremiah 23:26).** They only spoke prophecies that were favorable to their "viewers." Now contrast that to what the Lord's prophet, Jeremiah, said: **"You shall go to Babylon, and there you shall die, and be buried there, you and all your friends, to whom you have prophesied lies" (see Jeremiah 20:6).**

AS GOES THE PROPHETIC, SO GOES THE NATION

Elisha had become sick with the illness of which he would die. Then Joash the king of Israel came down to him, and wept over his face, and said, "O my father, my father, the chariots of Israel and their horsemen!"

And Elisha said to him, "Take a bow and some arrows." So he took himself a bow and some arrows. Then he said to the king of Israel, "Put your hand on the bow." So he put his hand on it, and Elisha put his hands on the king's hands. And he said, "Open the east window"; and he opened it. Then Elisha said, "Shoot"; and he shot. And he said, "The arrow of the Lord's deliverance and the arrow of deliverance from Syria; for you must strike the Syrians at Aphek till you have destroyed them." Then he said, "Take the arrows"; so he took them. And he said to the king of Israel, "Strike the ground"; so he struck three times, and stopped. And the man of God was angry with him, and said, "You should have struck five or six times; then you would have struck Syria till you had destroyed it! But now you will strike Syria only three times."

Then Elisha died, and they buried him (2 Kings 13:14-20).

Elisha represented the prophetic of his day. Elisha was sick with a sickness unto death. The prophetic ministry has often become sick and has not always functioned in healthy ways. The prophetic can become sick. There was also trouble in the nation of Israel when the prophetic became sick and was about to die, and we can see some of these same parallels in America today.

Sin and evil marked Joash's reign. He was a false worshiper of the one true God. Though he did not worship other gods, he did not worship God in the way He wanted to be worshiped. When Joash was dealing with all these things and the prophetic was dying in the nation, he knelt down over Elisha and said, **"The**

chariots of Israel and their horsemen!" It's pretty profound that Joash said the same words to Elisha just before he died that Elisha once said to Elijah just before he was taken up in a chariot of fire: **"My father, my father, the chariots of Israel and its horsemen!" (see 2 Kings 2:12)**

Joash recognized the strength of Israel was in the presence of a strong, healthy prophetic ministry. He mourned to see that strength slip from the earth. Victory was on the side of Israel whenever there was a strong and healthy prophetic ministry. He connected their prosperity to the strength of chariots, which also represented the prophetic. Joash realized that the nation's decline was connected to unhealthy prophetic people.

What you have invested in by reading this book is desperately needed in America and in the world. America has a prophetic call, and we need a healthy prophetic ministry. Our nation and world need us. Our nation and world suffer when there are not strong prophetic voices speaking to our leaders and to our people. Joash connected the sickness and death of the prophetic to his nation's decline.

I believe God is raising up mature prophets today who understand the power of unity. Many are feeling the call to become part of a prophetic company who will be of value to our cities, states, nation, and world. We often hear, "As goes the church, so goes the nation." There is much truth in that statement. The church is built on the foundation of the apostles and prophets (see Ephesians 2:20), so when the prophetic is not part of the church's foundation, the church cannot be built as it should.

If the decline of the prophetic ministry is connected to the decline of a nation, then a strong prophetic ministry makes a nation strong. We need politicians and educators who understand that when true prophetic people arise, so does the nation. We must speak to the secrets of men's hearts. Even evil politicians should mourn when the prophets are not accessible or available. They also need someone who can speak on behalf of the Lord and speak prophetic guidance to their lives. The church must realize, once again, the importance of prophetic ministry.

Joash was concerned that the true strength of Israel was about to depart, so Elisha used the illustration of arrows shot through an open window to represent the arrows of God's deliverance and presence still being in Israel. All Joash had to do was shoot in faith. It was an ancient custom to shoot an arrow toward a country you were about to invade. Through this prophetic act, a connection was made between shooting an arrow toward the east and striking the Syrians, and God's deliverance. There was no intended target. Elisha was simply giving Joash "hands-on" training in how to fight against the Syrians. Elisha literally put his hands on Joash's hands as he gripped the bow. This prophetically symbolized great spiritual activity. The arrows represented strikes against their Syrian enemies, and the arrows Joash struck the ground with prophetically represented victories over God's enemies.

He only struck the ground three times, which determined the number and size of victories they would have. Victory was literally within Joash's grip. "Striking the ground" meant shooting arrows without knowing where they would land toward an undefined target. Joash limited Israel to only three victories. Personally, I would have kept shooting until the Lord told me to stop. These arrows were like prophetic ministry and prayer.

LESSONS FROM PROPHETIC EVANGELISM

It takes faith to keep striking the ground without knowing the results or where the arrows might land. When you don't know, keep shooting, keep aiming, and keep firing, even if you don't know where your prayers or prophetic words will land, or if they'll even hit the target. God is looking for a people of faith who don't need prodding to fire every arrow they have, even without a defined target.

Joash hesitated. We also hesitate. We worry about "missing the mark," so we don't give a prophetic word to that person at Walmart whom we believed needed healing. Just pull out those arrows and keep firing! It still moves the Spirit and ultimately determines our number of victories. Perhaps you didn't have a specific target, or you felt limited about going "all out" in prayer. Pray anyway! God is looking for a people of faith who will not be bound by fear or hesitation. It takes faith to keep shooting and aiming when you cannot see the bullseye or even the target. The point is to obey and keep shooting. Our words may fall straight to the ground, but God still blesses the fact that we're willing to shoot. We must be willing to go "all out" and give it our best shot!

"Having then gifts differing according to the grace that is given to us, <u>let us use them</u>: if prophecy, let us prophesy in proportion to our faith" (Romans 12:6). Did you catch that? **"Let us use them."** In other words, don't leave your arrows in the quiver! If it's prophecy, let us prophesy according to our faith. If we only have three-arrow faith, that is the level of victory we will have. We shoot according to the proportion of our faith. Little faith, little victory. **"O you of little faith" (see Matthew 14:31).**

Notice Elisha never put a limit on the number of arrows Joash could shoot. We all aim and shoot according to the proportion of our faith. Don't limit God's ability to work through you. Just keep shooting until the enemy is defeated. Shooting arrows requires aim and effort. Shooting arrows must be done through open windows without knowing the exact outcome. Our targets are only known **"by faith" (see Hebrews 11).** Joash's arrows were ineffective because he did not strike enough, reflecting his lack of faith in the process. Shooting arrows is about strategic *kairos* moments, and sometimes when those moments pass, they're gone forever.

How many times have we felt a prompting and didn't use an arrow? Why should He give us more? Failing to use all his arrows not only hurt Joash but also an entire nation. Those were lost victories for Israel. Because Joash did not seize his prophetic moment, Israel could only enjoy three victories over the Syrians, when they could have enjoyed many more. We are all facing a moment of destiny right now in our lives, but because some are afraid to make the move, take the step, and shoot the arrow, we're not really sure if we will reach our destination. Don't miss this moment!

How many times have we felt we should share a dream with someone that might help them? We must follow the promptings of the Holy Spirit. We are stealing healing. How many people are missing out in life because we failed to respond when a window was opened to us? We shortchanged ourselves and robbed others of their victories as well. How many times have we settled for less than God's best? How many times have we left arrows in our quivers? "Walking in the Spirit" means following the promptings of the Holy Spirit. How many and how big would Israel's victories have been had Joash kept striking the ground until Elisha told him to stop?

Keep shooting. Keep practicing the prophetic. Keep praying. Keep practicing prophetic activations until you learn. Keep aiming to attain more faith. Keep shooting to hit the target. Bold, courageous actions (not timid ones) bring big victories. Keep shooting for the mark and keep aiming for the target for the kingdom of God.

Joash's lack of faith was manifested in his half-hearted effort to smite the ground, just like us and our excuses: "I stopped shooting because I'm more reserved." "I stopped shooting because

I didn't want to be presumptuous." "I stopped shooting because my words aren't accurate or high-level enough." "I stopped shooting because I didn't want to make a scene or be perceived as weird." "I stopped shooting because I didn't get enough 'hands-on' training." "I stopped shooting because I didn't receive enough encouragement." Don't wait for your pastor to hear from God for you. Take the training wheels off. Get your arrows, grab your bow, and shoot anyway!

Sometimes we can be limited by our church environment if it's not healthy or sympathetic to the prophetic. Consequently, some have hung their bows and arrows. Get out your bow and arrows and let God use you again!

For since the creation of the world His invisible attributes are clearly seen, being understood by the things that are made, even His eternal power and Godhead, so that they are <u>without excuse</u> (Romans 1:20).

But solid food belongs to those who are of full age, that is, those who by reason of use <u>have their senses exercised</u> to discern both good and evil (Hebrews 5:14).

These Scriptures clearly tell us that those who are spiritually mature have developed their spiritual senses to see, hear, taste, smell, touch, and discern in the spirit realm, and those who have not are without excuse. It is by reason of use or practice that our senses or sensibilities are exercised. That is the purpose of prophetic activations.

If we have unused arrows, we should not wonder why our prophetic gifts have not developed as much as we would like. Keep shooting! Keep doing those prophetic activations. Keep shooting out the window, even if you don't know where your arrows will land. Just obey the Lord, knowing that shooting prophetic arrows brings victories.

LESSONS FROM PROPHETIC ACTIVATIONS

God can speak in many ways, and some of those ways can offend religious minds. The following examples of prophetic activations represent just some of the ways God can speak and relate to us. These methods vary from person to person based on our prophetic filters, which is how God speaks to us personally. I encourage you to practice these among your church peers, small group, family, and friends. For example, God may highlight or reveal to you:

1. **An object from your environmental surroundings** (floors or carpet: "You've been walked on." Chairs: "God wants you to rest." Walls: "God wants to break down barriers in your life." Ceiling: "God wants to break through a glass ceiling in your life." Light: "God sees you as a light to others.")

2. **The face of a person you know** (as you begin to describe a person you know, God may reveal a common or similar name, work background, personality trait, characteristic, or life event.)

3. **A Bible character** (this may reveal spiritual gifts, ministries, character traits, common backgrounds, interests, or employment.)

4. **A scriptural phrase ("Only be strong and very courageous" (see Joshua 1:7).** Like Joshua, God wants you to focus on building your faith in God and eliminating fear from your life.")

5. **An animal** (a courageous lion, gentle lamb, peaceful dove, worker ox, seer eagle, eagle flying above storms, or a giraffe reaching to the heavens.)

6. **A famous song title or lyric** ("Amazing Grace": "God wants to save you." "Unchained Melody": "God hungers for your love." "You've Lost That Lovin' Feeling": "You used to follow God, but you lost your first love." "The Twist": "An unexpected twist is coming to your life." "You Light Up My Life": "God wants to give you hope to carry on.")

7. **A building** (The Eiffel Tower that lights the sky, a skyscraper that reaches to the heavens, a beautiful cathedral that draws people to God, or a lighthouse that saves lives.)

8. **A career** (a shepherd who cares for others; a farmer who plants, waters, and produces a harvest; a carpenter who builds shelters, furniture, utensils for use; an artist-craftsman who designs and creates beauty.)

9. **Objects of nature** (Rock: "You're solid and immoveable." Water: "You're flowing, nourishing, refreshing." Tree: "You're planted, flexible, a shelter to others." Fire: "You spread warmth, you're wild and free." Flower: "You're beautiful, uplifting, and comforting.")

DISCUSSION QUESTIONS

1. What did the Samaritan woman learn about prophetic ministry? What were some of the results of Jesus' ministry to her at the well that day?

2. What can we learn from Jesus about correction and calling out sin in people's lives? What can we learn from our current culture about correction and calling out sin in people's lives?

3. What are some prophetic "dos and don'ts" we learn from Jesus' ministry to the woman at the well?

4. What are some of the "dos and don'ts" can we learn from Agabus' personal prophecy to Paul?

5. One of the most common reasons for rejection of personal prophecies is "confirmation bias." Define "confirmation bias" and explain why this must be addressed in the body of Christ.

6. Name some of the advantages and benefits of receiving international prophecies and warnings.

7. In 2 Kings 13, what were some of the lessons Joash learned from Elisha about prophetic ministry and the state or condition of a nation? What is the correlation between them?

8. How does Joash's failure to keep shooting arrows at Elisha's instruction correlate to prophetic evangelism?

9. God is really unlimited in the ways He can speak and relate to us. Can you think of any other prophetic activations? What prophetic activation is your personal favorite and why?

PRAYING INTO
the Prophetic

When He had been baptized, Jesus came up immediately from the water; and behold, <u>the heavens were opened to Him</u>, and He saw the Spirit of God descending like a dove and alighting upon Him. And suddenly <u>a voice came from heaven</u>, saying, "This is My beloved Son, in whom I am well pleased" (Matthew 3:16-17).

THE HEAVENS WERE OPENED TO JESUS

"A voice came from heaven." This is prophetic revelation— hearing and discerning the voice of God. **"This is My beloved Son, in whom I am well pleased."** The Lord speaks more than we realize, and we often mistake His voice for our thoughts. Jesus was thirty years old and had not performed a public miracle up to this point. Something caused the heavens to be opened to Him. This is important. It began with **"behold."** Every believer should desire to live under open heavens. This should be our goal, because the Spirit of God descended when the heavens were opened. They saw a deluge of God's Spirit, they clearly heard the voice of God, and Jesus' Sonship was established.

Likewise, when the heavens are opened to us, we will see an outpouring of God's Spirit, we will clearly hear God's voice, and a declaration of our sonship will be established. This is the first type of open heaven, which is also called a "holy visitation." There are different types of open heavens.

> **<u>Oh, that You would rend the heavens!</u> That You would come down! That the mountains might shake at Your presence— as fire burns brushwood, as fire causes water to boil—to make Your name known to Your adversaries, that the nations may tremble at Your presence! (Isaiah 64:1-2)**

What happens when God comes down from heaven? The mountains shake at His presence. Fire comes down and burns. His name is made known to His adversaries, and the nations tremble at His presence. This can happen to an individual, or it can happen worldwide, and every knee will bow.

We must desire a mighty visitation in our lives from the Lord. We must pray for an open heaven over our lives, families, churches, cities, and nations. If there is one thing the world needs, it is open heavens to bring reformation, melt nations, and cause trembling at His presence. The world needs to experience the fear of the Lord once again.

"So then faith comes by hearing, and hearing by the word of God" (Romans 10:17). If our churches emphasize healing, we will grow in healing. The word of God is released by the Holy Spirit on that subject. Faith comes by hearing God's word on a subject. We receive what we preach. His word will not return void (see Isaiah 55:11). If we preach the truth about open heavens, we will receive faith for it. Why not believe now to receive faith for legitimate open heavens over our lives? We want heaven rending, not brass heavens (see Deuteronomy 28:23). We want to see God burst through over our cities, nations, regions, lives, and ministries.

PRACTICING HIS PRESENCE

I have never been hungrier for God's manifest presence than I am right now. Hebrews 12:2 says, **"Looking unto Jesus, the author and finisher of our faith."** The Greek word translated *looking* here means "to gaze, stargaze, stare at," or "become acquainted with." Psalm 91:1 says, **"He who dwells in the secret place of the Most High shall abide under the shadow of the Almighty."** We want to abide under His shadow.

My prayer is Psalm 27:4: **"One thing I have desired of the Lord, that will I seek: that I may dwell in the house of the Lord all the days of my life, to behold the beauty of the Lord, and to inquire in His temple."** Would you like to join me in casting your gaze on the Lord? Would you like Him to rend the heavens for you, so you can experience an authentic breakthrough? Look!

The Practice of the Presence of God by Brother Lawrence is a key book. We must sit quietly and wait. This is one of the most important practices we can do; have our gaze locked on Jesus. It's called, "silent prayer" or "prayer of the heart." If your entire idea of prayer is yelling at God and being fervent, I want you to know there's a place for sitting and waiting on the Lord, and this can be the most difficult thing to do in our busy society. We don't have to do all the talking in prayer. Sit and wait with your gaze fixed on Jesus!

Isaiah 40:31 says, **"But those who wait on the Lord shall renew their strength; they shall mount up with wings like eagles, they shall run and not be weary, they shall walk and not faint."** There is an element of quiet, silent prayer that gives us eagles' wings. The eagle or eagle's eye is symbolic in Scripture of the prophetic. The eagle is made for high altitudes. Strength for the race comes when we wait on the Lord. **"Let us run with endurance the race that is set before us" (see Hebrews 12:1).**

If the heavens can be opened to us, it only stands to reason they can also be closed over us and over our nation. The heavens can also be open over a city yet closed over a nation, closed over a city yet open over a church, or closed over a family yet open over an individual. This can even happen in the same house and under the same roof, where some do not seek the Lord, while others live in His presence. Jesus alluded to this when He said, **"I did not come to bring peace but a sword. For I have come to set a man against his father, a daughter against her mother, and daughter-in-law against her mother-in-law" (see Matthew 10:34-35).**

Jesus faced opposition from the Pharisees, Sadducees, and religious leaders, yet He lived under open heavens and took revival with Him wherever He went. Religious spirits are often the greatest opposition to what God is trying to do on earth. People will often criticize what makes them feel insecure. Don't help the devil by criticizing others. We have enough friendly fire and enemy fire hitting our fellow Christians without us adding to it.

People want to go and stay wherever the heavens are open, whether over a city, a church, a family, or an individual. After the heavens opened to Jesus in Matthew 3:16, everything changed. The greatest healing, deliverance, and miracle ministry on earth happened after that. John said, if all the things Jesus did were written down, the world could not contain all the books (see John 21:25). Jesus took revival with Him wherever He went, and we want to do the same.

OPEN ACCESS TO HEAVEN

When the heavens are opened to us, we have access to everything in heaven and a free flow of God's supernatural grace. If we have faith for it, we can experience it, but we must believe it is for us. Paul wrote about the "riches of His glory" (see Romans 9:23; Ephesians 1:18, 3:16) and His glory *is* rich. We need to pray for a release of "the riches of His glory" in our lives. We can receive more of the riches of His glory, which is already ours. The cross paid for it. It's like accomplishing much without any heavy labor and without breaking a sweat. It's functioning from a posture of rest. When we live under open heavens, we carry heaven's blueprint wherever we go and can freely access revelation by faith.

After these things I looked, and behold, <u>a door standing open in heaven</u>. And the first voice which I heard was like a trumpet speaking with me, saying, "Come up here, and I will show you things which must take place after this."

Immediately I was in the Spirit; and behold, a throne set in heaven, and One sat on the throne (Revelation 4:1).

John saw an open door in heaven, and as far as we know, this door was never shut. It's still available to us, and it's continually getting easier to enter this realm. We can practice this all the time —praying in the Spirit, quieting ourselves, opening ourselves to receive open heaven realities, visions, and dreams—until we literally access it. Each time we do, it gets easier. The more practice, the more access. In the garden, Adam and Eve could be in both places at the same time—naming the animals *and* walking and talking with God.

Practice going to the open heavens. Open the door by faith. The occult practices this their way, and it brings an evil presence. There's an increase in the occult in this season, but we have access to the Revelation 4:1 door. Jesus is the door to the open heavens. Open heavens can also open finances.

OPEN HEAVENS OVER OUR FINANCES

"Now it shall come to pass, if you diligently obey the voice of the Lord your God, to observe carefully all His commandments which I command you today, that the Lord your God will set you high above all nations of the earth. And all these blessings shall come upon you and overtake you, because you obey the voice of the Lord your God:

"Blessed shall you be in the city, and blessed shall you be in the country.

"Blessed shall be the fruit of your body, the produce of your ground and the increase of your herds, the increase of your cattle and the offspring of your flocks.

"Blessed shall be your basket and your kneading bowl.

"Blessed shall you be when you come in, and blessed shall you be when you go out.

"The Lord will cause your enemies who rise against you to be defeated before your face; they shall come out against you one way and flee before you seven ways.

"The Lord will command the blessing on you in your storehouses and in all to which you set your hand, and He will bless you in the land which the Lord your God is giving you.

"The Lord will establish you as a holy people to Himself, just as He has sworn to you, if you keep the commandments of the Lord your God and walk in His ways. Then all peoples of the earth shall see that you are called by the name of the Lord, and they shall be afraid of you. And the Lord will grant you plenty of goods, in the fruit of your body, in the increase of your livestock, and in the produce of your ground, in the land of which the Lord swore to your fathers to give you.

<u>The Lord will open to you His good treasure, the heavens,</u> to give the rain to your land in its season, and to bless all the work of your hand. You shall lend to many nations, but you shall not borrow. And the Lord will make you the head and not the tail; you shall be above only, and not be beneath, if you heed the commandments of the Lord your God, which I command you today, and are careful to observe them. So you shall not turn aside from any of the words which I command you this day, to the right or the left, to go after other gods to serve them" (Deuteronomy 28:1-14).

Blessings shall come upon you in the city and in the country. The Lord will open to you the good treasure of His heavens. These are the open heavens. These are not "prosperity gospel" Scriptures; this is about an obedient lifestyle that can maintain open heavens and create prosperity in our lives, *including* financial prosperity.

Tithes and offerings are not just Old Testament concepts. They are part of receiving the blessings of the Lord. Abraham paid tithes to Melchizedek before the old covenant law of Moses was established. The Jews tithed their cattle because that was their monetary system. Our monetary system today in the United States is the dollar.

"Will a man rob God? Yet you have robbed Me! But you say, 'In what way have we robbed You?' In tithes and offerings. You are cursed with a curse, for you have robbed Me, even this whole nation. Bring all the tithes into the storehouse, that there may be food in My house, and try Me now in this," says the Lord of hosts, "<u>If I will not open for you the windows of heaven</u> and pour out for you such blessing that there will not be room enough to receive it.

"And I will rebuke the devourer for your sakes, so that he will not destroy the fruit of your ground, nor shall the vine fail to bear fruit for you in the field," says the Lord of hosts; "And all nations will call you blessed, for you will be a delightful land," says the Lord of hosts" (Malachi 3:8-12).

The Word of God is true from culture to culture and generation to generation. He says to try Him. He said, **"Try me now in this ... if I will not open for you the windows of heaven."** This is also part of the open heavens experience. Many people who struggle financially have a poverty mentality and do not tithe.

There are four promises under a financial open heaven. Jesus used negative power only once—on the tree that did not produce fruit (see Mark 11:12-14). It took nutrients from the soil and energy from the sun but did not give anything back. It was breaking a law of nature, and such practices are accursed. We must produce fruit, and we must keep storing food in the storehouse that feeds us. Some people have perverted this truth, but this is no reason for us to stop obeying God.

God will open heaven's windows and pour us out blessings we cannot contain. Why? So, He can work through us, heal the sick through us, and pour out rivers of living water through us to others (see John 7:38). He will also rebuke the devourer for our sakes, and all nations will call us blessed.

BRASS HEAVENS

This has everything to do with open heavens and receiving from His treasure, heaven. Some Christians cannot go deeper in the prophetic because their heavens are like brass, but if we want more, we can receive more. If we want to go deeper, we must have open heavens.

> **In the six hundredth year of Noah's life, in the second month, the seventeenth day of the month, on that day all the fountains of the great deep were broken up, and <u>the windows of heaven were opened.</u> And the rain was on the earth forty days and forty nights (Genesis 7:11-12).**

Even in Genesis, the heavens were opened. The moment the fountains of the deep opened up, the heavens were opened, and there was an outpouring. Do you want God's deep streams to spring up? The prophetic community needs pastoring and mentoring. That is what Elijah was to Elisha.

Psalm 78:23-24 says, **"Yet He had commanded the clouds above, and <u>opened the doors of heaven,</u> had rained down manna on them to eat, and given them of the bread of heaven."** Here again are the doors of heaven, like in Revelation 4, when the doors of heaven opened. The first thing that came raining down from heaven was manna. Manna was the most frequent biblical manifestation of open heavens. For six days, they gathered manna. We need to live on today's manna, not yesterday's manna. Manna represents fresh revelation from heaven.

Some people live under partially opened heavens or only in certain areas of their lives. Others live under closed heavens. Still others live under completely open heavens, like in Psalm 78. When heaven's doors are opened, fresh manna and bread are released. Feast on Jesus, the Bread from heaven (see John 6:41).

Fresh manna represents deeper prophetic encounters, prophetic secrets, and revelations.

What do brass heavens look like? Deuteronomy 28:15 describes the opposite of open heavens. **"If you do *not* obey the voice of the Lord your God ... all these curses will come upon you and overtake you" (see Deuteronomy 28:15**, emphasis added). However, Jesus made it possible for these curses to be broken off our lives.

A brass heaven is when the earth does not yield its fruit, when things dry up financially, when people stop getting saved, when God's favor seems to dry up, when we face consistent resistance, and when everything becomes an uphill battle. Deuteronomy 28:23 says, **"<u>And your heavens which are over your head shall be bronze</u>, and the earth which is under you shall be iron" (Deuteronomy 28:23).** The *last* thing we want is brass heavens and an iron earth.

There's something about living a life of obedience that keeps the heavens open to us. Jesus lived a life that flowed from the Holy Spirit. He was the Tree of Life. In Him we can live Spirit-led lives the same way He did. Legalism shuts up the heavens. It can cause dead churches and shut up the heavens, like it did for Adam and Eve.

How do we get out from under brass heavens? Any atmosphere we constantly nurture will become our environment. Cultivate your atmosphere. The more consistently we seek the Lord and believe by faith to receive from Him, we produce a consistent environment of open heavens like Jesus experienced. Jesus lived under open heavens. As adopted sons and daughters, we should aim high. Struggles may come our way under open heavens, but we have authority to overcome them.

Jesus lived an obedient life. Repentance and obedience can open up closed heavens. After John the Baptist's ministry of repentance, Jesus was baptized, and His obedience to the Father opened up the heavens. Jesus' life of obedience kept the heavens opened to Him. **"He learned obedience by the things which He suffered" (see Hebrews 5:8).** His grace also works in our favor if we remain humble.

Jesus' miracle ministry was the result of heaven being opened and remaining open over Him. He healed the sick, delivered the oppressed, and was constantly shown what the Father was doing (see John 5:19). He had a revelatory experience—as opposed to the Pharisees, who were religious, skeptical, and critical.

OPEN HEAVENS OF REVELATION

What do open heavens of consistent revelation look like? It's a sign of the last days outpouring—visions, dreams, words, insights into world events, prophecies, and being watchmen on the walls.

After these things I looked, and behold, <u>a door standing open in heaven</u>. And the first voice which I heard was like a trumpet speaking with me, saying, "Come up here, and I will show you things which must take place after this" (Revelation 4:1).

"<u>Now I saw heaven opened</u>, and behold, a white horse. And He who sat on him was called Faithful and True, and in righteousness He judges and makes war" (Revelation 19:11).

Now it came to pass in the thirtieth year, in the fourth month, on the fifth day of the month, as I was among the captives by the River Chebar, that <u>the heavens were opened and I saw visions of God</u> (Ezekiel 1:1).

This type of open heaven brings more visions and revelations.

> **The next day, as they went on their journey and drew near the city, Peter went up on the housetop to pray, about the sixth hour. Then he became very hungry and wanted to eat; but while they made ready, <u>he fell into a trance and saw heaven opened</u> and an object like a great sheet bound at the four corners, descending to him and let down to the earth. In it were all kinds of four-footed animals of the earth, wild beasts, creeping things, and birds of the air. And a voice came to him, "Rise, Peter; kill and eat" (Acts 10:9-13).**

Trances are also tied to open heavens. Peter was in a trance and saw the heavens opened. It was a revelation about Jesus bringing the Gentiles into the new covenant.

How can we create an environment of open heavens? By waiting on the Lord. **"But solid food belongs to those who are of full age, that is, those who by reason of use have their senses exercised to discern both good and evil" (Hebrews 5:14).** We mature our spiritual senses by waiting on the Lord. **"They soon forgot His works; <u>they did not wait for His counsel</u>, but lusted exceedingly in the wilderness, and tested God in the desert. And He gave them their request, but sent leanness into their soul" (Psalm 106:13-15).**

> **Now the boy Samuel ministered to the Lord before Eli. And <u>the word of the Lord was rare in those days; there was no widespread revelation</u>. And it came to pass at that time, while Eli was lying down in his place, and when his eyes had begun to grow so dim that he could not see, and before the lamp of God went out in the tabernacle of the Lord where the ark of God was, and while Samuel was lying down, that the Lord called Samuel. And he answered, "Here I am!" So he ran to Eli and said, "Here I am, for you called me."**

And he said, "I did not call; lie down again." And he went and lay down.

Then the Lord called yet again, "Samuel!"

So Samuel arose and went to Eli, and said, "Here I am, for you called me." He answered, "I did not call, my son; lie down again." (<u>Now Samuel did not yet know the Lord, nor was the word of the Lord yet revealed to him.</u>)

And the Lord called Samuel again the third time. So he arose and went to Eli, and said, "Here I am, for you did call me" (1 Samuel 3:1-8).

At this point, the word of the Lord had not yet been revealed to Samuel. However, like Samuel, the word of the Lord can and will be revealed to us. Eli and his sons were backslidden; there was no open vision. Eli laid down, his eyes waxed dim, and the lamp went out in the temple. The Holy Spirit was no longer moving.

Then God raised up a new prophet, Samuel, who prophesied along the Messianic line, and anointed David as king. Samuel was lying down near the ark, which represented the manifest presence of God. Leadership was asleep, but Samuel positioned himself in a posture of rest to soak in the manifest presence of God. Prophetic revelation and vision were then restored through a boy. If you want to experience open heavens in your finances, family, job, or your personal level of revelation, faith comes by hearing and now you know how.

OPEN HEAVENS TO GOD'S THRONE ROOM

After these things I looked, and behold, a door standing open in heaven. And the first voice which I heard was like a trumpet speaking with me, saying, "<u>Come up here, and I will show you things which must take place after this</u>" (Revelation 4:1).

Here John received an invitation to God's throne room. He saw a door and heard a voice. He saw and heard in the spirit realm. Our senses are rooted in our spirit beings and will continue long after we leave our physical bodies. Proof of this is Jesus' parable of the rich man and Lazarus (see Luke 16:19-31). Our senses can be trained outside our physical bodies.

Immediately I was in the Spirit; and behold, a throne set in heaven, and One sat on the throne. And He who sat there was like a jasper and a sardius stone in appearance; and there was a rainbow around the throne, in appearance like an emerald. Around the throne were twenty-four thrones, and on the thrones I saw twenty-four elders sitting, clothed in white robes; and they had crowns of gold on their heads. And from the throne proceeded lightnings, thunderings, and voices. Seven lamps of fire were burning before the throne, which are the seven Spirits of God.

Before the throne there was a sea of glass, like crystal. And in the midst of the throne, and around the throne, were four living creatures full of eyes in front and in back. The first living creature was like a lion, the second living creature like a calf, the third living creature had a face like a man, and the fourth living creature was like a flying eagle. The four living creatures, each having six wings, were full of eyes around and within. And they do not rest day or night, saying: "Holy, holy, holy, Lord God Almighty, Who was and is and is to come!" (Revelation 4:2-8)

Throne room encounters will be opened to us if we receive them by faith. John saw an open door in heaven, and as far as we know, this door was never shut. So, I want to provoke you to access these things of the Spirit by faith. Spiritual perception is based on the purity of our hearts and rooted in the soil of our inner thought lives. Pure hearts are essential to this.

In the throne room was a sea of glass. This is to reflect what is there in us. What we see in heaven, God wants to reflect on earth. The twenty-four elders were seated around the throne. The four living creatures, of which Ezekiel also spoke (see Ezekiel 1:15), are interesting. They were full of eyes, in front and behind, and around and within. **"Blessed are the pure in heart, for they shall see God" (Matthew 5:8).** There is a clear connection between pure hearts and spiritual eyes being opened. Greater throne room realities are discovered when we pursue holiness. The Holy of Holies is the core of the tabernacle. The further we go in the tabernacle and into God's throne room, the more holiness is needed. However, we cannot manufacture it; it's a work of the Holy Spirit in our hearts.

We should all seek open visions of God's throne room. Heavenly dreams, angels, throne room realities, and more are all available to us. They are received by faith. This means we must first believe they are for us. The four beasts that John saw are a deeper truth. These living creatures were closest to God's throne and like the four faces of God—the lion (apostolic anointing), the sacrificial calf (Christ), the man (Jesus), and the flying eagle (prophetic anointing). The four closest to the throne had the most eyes to see in front, behind, around, and within. This represents the open, all-inclusive vision of God's presence. The closer we get to God's throne, the more we'll see, and the more revelation and spiritual perception we'll receive.

The Lord is seated on the throne. If you've ever met the Lord, it's because your spirit went to His throne. John 3:3 says we were "born again." This means "born from above." Through the Holy Spirit, our spirits are now seated with Christ on His throne in heavenly places (see Ephesians 2:6). Here, we can see, pray, and live in a heavenly realm. We're no longer living from our souls but from our spirits which were quickened and made alive at salvation. From this position we are seated with Christ in heavenly places.

If we as believers are spiritually positioned with Christ in heavenly places, why would heavenly throne room realities be shut off from us? Revelation 3:21 takes this even one step further: **"To him who overcomes I will grant to sit with Me on My throne."** We have been given dominion over our thoughts, actions, and emotions. According to 1 John 5:18, we can even determine how close the enemy can get near to us. Because of our heavenly position in Christ Jesus, we have been given authority to rule and reign in this life. Start proclaiming the promises of God from where your spirit lives, where God's presence is, and where open heavens are, not from where your soul lives.

SPIRITUAL EYES AND PURE HEARTS

The closer we get to God's throne, the more our spiritual eyes will see. The four living creatures were full of eyes. They were called *living* creatures because they were so close to the Lord that His light and life maintained theirs. Jesus came that we might have life and have it more abundantly (see John 10:10). We receive light and life by feeding from the presence of God. Through Him we can think, discern, hear, smell, taste, and feel heaven. The mind of Christ fuses with our vision to reveal what we cannot see through our narrow, earthly perceptions.

Through Him we can see from the front, behind, outside, and inside. We can see future events in front of us, past events behind us, and can even look within and measure our internal hearts and lives. 1 Corinthians 2:10 says, **"But God has revealed them to us through His Spirit. For the Spirit searches all things, yes, the deep things of God."** We are close enough to God to even search the deep things of God.

To be prophetic, we *need* eyes and being near to God even gives us eyes within. Those who live close to God's throne have eyes to monitor their internal motives, eyes to stand guard against sin. The slightest sin becomes magnified when we have eyes within. The four living creatures do not cease day or night to say, "Holy, holy, holy." With our spiritual eyes open, it's easy to worship and adore Him from our hearts. Worship is not a struggle when we encounter God's throne room.

Praise naturally flows from our lips because we are *that* close to His presence and majesty. How can we be *that* close to God and remain unresponsive? Even the dead are awakened in His presence. Even demons scream (see Mark 3:11) in His presence. How carnally minded can we be that, while even demons and rocks cry out in His presence (see Luke 19:40), we do not?

Those closest to the Lord praise the Lord the loudest in pure affection, loving God with all their heart, soul, mind, and strength. In John 1:47, **"Jesus saw Nathanael coming toward Him and said of him, 'Behold, an Israelite indeed, in whom is no deceit.'"** What kind of man must Nathanael have been for Jesus to say this? I'd like to meet a man "in whom is no deceit." We should all desire to be like him.

Nathanael had eyes within, which created a pure heart. That is why Jesus encountered him. He wants to encounter us, too. He wants us to experience throne room realities more than we do. God wants us to behold Him more than we do. It's about posturing our hearts and maintaining God's truth in our inward parts. When we cleave to God's truth inwardly, we will see it outwardly. Nathanael's spiritual eyes were quickly opened to Jesus because of the posture of his heart. *That* is spiritual perception.

Jesus told Nathanael, **"You will see greater things than these …. You shall see heaven open, and the angels of God ascending and descending on the Son of Man." (see John 1:50-51).** When we cling to truth inwardly, we will behold truth outwardly and expect to see heaven opened. Start praying, proclaiming, and expecting to see angels of God ascending and descending because you desire truth in your inward parts. We access our inheritance by faith. What if we saw heaven open and angels coming down? We can! Believe the promises of God. Jesus knew Nathanael would see angels ascending and descending because of his pure heart.

Every battle and temptation we face is so we can become overcomers. The fight is to see God in the heavenly realm. This is why we fight. We want pure hearts to see God and to see heaven open. Because of Nathaniel's honest heart, Jesus knew open visions were inevitable. Open visions are the consequences of truth in our inward parts. Those of us who fight against sin, hate falsehood, and pursue holiness must get back up even if we fall. Our struggles are only preparations for overcoming every worldly thing. The real fight is to keep our hearts pure before God because we want to see Him, and we want to see heaven open!

When our hearts become dull, we don't expect to see heaven open. Don't accept that as the norm. Many Christians see heaven as brass, as closed, but it's only closed to those whose hearts are brass. God wants us to have true spiritual vision.

"And it shall come to pass in the last days, says God, that I will pour out of My Spirit on all flesh; your sons and your daughters shall prophesy, your young men <u>shall see visions</u>, your old men shall dream dreams" (Acts 2:17). This was a sign of the Pentecostal outpouring. Some have denied this, saying those things were only for the first century. Ours is not a blind trust but a proven trust. Cessationists say, **"We walk by faith, not by sight" (see 2 Corinthians 5:7)** yet deny today's move of the Holy Spirit. But Paul said, **"While we do not look at the things that are seen, but at the things which are not seen" (see 2 Corinthians 4:18).**

THE HEAVENS WERE OPENED TO PAUL

Paul had a revelational perception of the spirit realm. He saw the eternal spiritual body that was waiting and prepared for him in the heavens (see 2 Corinthians 5:1, 4). Paul also saw a man caught up to the third heaven (speaking of himself in the third person) and was humble about it (see 2 Corinthians 12:3-5). This New Testament "man" was caught up to the third heaven and saw and heard things which were unlawful to repeat. I don't say this lightly, but I also want us to be caught up to such heavenly realities that, when we leave them, we won't be sure if we should share them.

Many of Paul's writings were about open visions. He met the Lord in a blinding light that opened his spiritual eyes. The light was so bright and clear that it blinded him. Jesus said, **"I am Jesus, whom you are persecuting" (see Acts 9:5).** Paul was physically blinded but, for the first time, his spiritual eyes were opened. I want to encounter Jesus like the four living creatures around God's throne. After this, instead of writing letters from the Sanhedrin to condemn Christians, Paul spent the rest of his life writing letters and calling Christians to this new kind of life.

Paul said that we behold the glory of the Lord with unveiled faces and are changed (see 2 Corinthians 3:18). This means we don't need to wait until we die to experience paradise. He said, **"But we have renounced the hidden things of shame" (see 2**

Corinthians 4:2). Then in 2 Corinthians 7:1, he writes, **"Therefore, having these promises, beloved, let us cleanse ourselves from all filthiness of the flesh and spirit, perfecting holiness in the fear of God."** In other words, from purified hearts and His perfected holiness come open visions of God's glory. We don't seek experiences; we seek a pure heart. Our experiences are the result of a purified heart. We're not chasing visions; we're chasing holiness. We're not trying to conjure up experiences; we simply want open heavens over us and refuse to accept brass heavens.

I want to see behind and in front of me. Don't look at past disappointments or shame. See future solutions before those problems even hit earth. See the headlines before they appear in the newspaper. What a tremendous inheritance we have of open heavens.

DISCUSSION QUESTIONS

1. What do you think caused the heavens to be opened to Jesus?

2. In the same way, do you think all believers should look for and expect the heavens to be opened to them? Why or why not?

3. In your own words, define what it means to "practice the presence of God."

4. Explain how the heavens can be opened over a city but not a nation, over a church but not a city, or over an individual but not other family members within the same household.

5. In your own words, what does "open access" to heaven look like?

6. What are some ways we can ensure "open heavens" over our finances?

7. What do "brass heavens" look like? How can we get out from under this?

8. How can we create an "open heavens" environment of consistent revelations and visitations from the Lord? Explain.

9. In John 1, what did Jesus say to Nathanael that equated spiritual eyes and spiritual visions with pure hearts? Can you think of other Scriptures that say the same thing?

10. In what ways were the heavens also opened to the apostle Paul?

"God has opened up a way for us to access the heavenly realms."

PROTOCOLS OF
the Prophetic

Though I speak with the tongues of men and of angels, but have not love, I have become sounding brass or a clanging cymbal. And though I have the gift of prophecy, and understand all mysteries and all knowledge, and though I have all faith, so that I could remove mountains, but have not love, I am nothing. And though I bestow all my goods to feed the poor, and though I give my body to be burned, but have not love, it profits me nothing.

Love suffers long and is kind; love does not envy; love does not parade itself, is not puffed up; does not behave rudely, does not seek its own, is not provoked, thinks no evil; does not rejoice in iniquity, but rejoices in the truth; bears all things, believes all things, hopes all things, endures all things.

<u>Love never fails. But whether there are prophecies, they will fail</u>; whether there are tongues, they will cease; whether there is knowledge, it will vanish away. For we know in part and we prophesy in part. But when that which is perfect has come, then that which is in part will be done away (1 Corinthians 13:1-10).

Love never fails, and anything that never fails is perfect. However, prophecies can and will fail.

When I was a child, I spoke as a child, I understood as a child, I thought as a child; but when I became a man, I put away childish things. For now we see in a mirror, dimly, but then face to face. Now I know in part, but then I shall know just as I also am known.

And now abide faith, hope, love, these three; but the greatest of these is love (1 Corinthians 13:11-13).

THE PROPHETIC PERFECTED IN LOVE

In 1 Corinthians 12, Paul wrote about spiritual gifts. In 1 Corinthians 13, he wrote about love in relation to spiritual gifts. In 1 Corinthians 14, he wrote about the administration of spiritual gifts in the church. Chapter 13 begins with Paul writing about spiritual gifts, **"Though I speak with the tongues of men and of angels."** The Corinthians were enamored with spiritual gifts, especially the gift of tongues. Paul said these gifts were incomplete and incapable of fulfilling their purpose without love.

We can actually speak with the tongues of men and of angels, but without love, it's just noise. We cannot be in a state of spiritual immaturity and without love, and still function in the gifts like we should. Speaking in tongues, if we are not mature, can cause messes in churches. Some of the most dangerous people in church history were spiritually gifted yet not made perfect in love. People may be spiritually gifted, but if they stop growing in love, the fallout can be noisy church splits, or worse.

There are nine gifts of the Spirit, and there are nine fruit of the Spirit to balance out those gifts. The Corinthians overemphasized the gifts but were underdeveloped in the fruit. This is also now happening among Pentecostal and Charismatic churches, or as Josiah Gregory once said, "People of little religion are always noisy; he who has not the love of God and man filling his heart is like an empty wagon coming violently down a hill: it makes a great noise, because there is nothing in it." Prophecy, faith, and knowledge to do miracles are likewise empty, incomplete, and irrelevant apart from love. The Corinthian Christians missed the goal and motive for the gifts of the Holy Spirit—love. Paul drew their attention back to that goal.

Quoting Jesus, Paul referred to the faith that can move mountains (see Matthew 17:20). How amazing would that be to have faith to do the impossible? Yet, even with such faith, we are nothing without love. Someone with great faith can move great mountains, but if they do not have love, they might set them down on top of someone or in someone else's path. This is not an issue of love versus gifts. Churches should never be forced to choose between love and the gifts of the Holy Spirit. Paul emphasized that the focus and goal of the gift is love, not gifts for their own sakes.

Self-sacrificial love is necessary. If we just want the gifts to stand out among our peers or to make headlines, that is wrong. The purpose of spiritual gifts working through faith is to help improve or better people's lives, connect them closer to God, manifest the kingdom of God, and make God's kingdom real to them. If our goal in the prophetic is to have encounters or to see angels, that is the motive of witchcraft and the occult. What makes the occult witchcraft is having selfish motives and desiring to make money by prophesying to people, then spending it on our own pleasures (see James 4:3).

What called Jesus to heal the sick, raise the dead, and heal the blind and the lame? Selfless love. We need a fresh baptism of His love, the kind the Father gave His Son. That is the fuel tank of spiritual gifts. Know your motives. We must do it for the sake of furthering God's kingdom in the lives of those around us.

Paul used the Greek word *agape* when speaking to the Corinthians. There are four Greek words for love, and we need to understand the difference. *Eros* means erotic, romantic, or sexual love. *Storge* refers to familial love, such as between a parent and child or between family members. *Phileo* speaks of deep friendship, brotherly love, partnership, or affection. *Phileo* is the highest love we can attain without God. Philadelphia means "the city of brotherly love." *Agape* is a deep, abiding love that never changes; a selfless love that gives without demanding or expecting anything in return; a love so great it can be given to the unlovable and unappealing and continue even when rejected. It gives because it wants to, and it loves without needing to receive.

Alan Redpath, in *Enduring Word Commentary*, says we get our English word "agony" from *agape*. He defines it as "the actual absorption of our being in one great passion." Strictly speaking, we cannot apply *agape* only to God's love, because the Bible teaches that men *agape* sin and the world (see John 3:19; 1 John 2:15). Some people love sin so much they hold on to it, like drugs or alcohol, though it may cost them their lives. *Agape* is a sacrificial, giving, absorbing love that has little to do with emotion. It is not warm and fuzzy. It is self-denial for the sake of another. You love someone so much you will give up your right to be right.

We can give our bodies to be burned or bestow all our goods to feed the poor, but without love, it profits nothing. We can suffer martyrdom or write a big check, and have it count for nothing because our motives are wrong. The rich, young ruler (see Matthew 19:16-30) whom Jesus told to give all his money to feed the poor and come follow Him, refused, and walked away sorrowful because he did not have *agape*. The Muslim who selfishly believes he will receive many virgins in heaven in return for his martyrdom does not have *agape*.

Prophecy will not have its full impact without love. Tongues may originate in the Spirit but will not have their full desired impact without *agape*. Without love, they are all in part and imperfect. *Agape* love as a fruit of the Spirit is meant to balance out the gifts.

TWO THINGS LOVE DOES

"Love suffers long..." "The Lord is not slack concerning His promises ... but is longsuffering toward us" (see 2 Peter 3:9). God puts up with us. We must do the same for those who disappoint or hurt us. We don't avenge ourselves even when we have opportunity.

"Love ... is kind." Love is displayed in simple yet wonderful acts of kindness. Children and even dogs receive us because they have discernment, but as we grow older, our childlike discernment can turn into suspicion. We must see kindness in people. Only God can give us *agape*. It is independent of feelings. Paul wrote about what love looks like in action.

EIGHT THINGS LOVE DOES NOT

"Love does not envy." This is one of the most damaging of all sins. It only causes hurt. Is envy a small sin? Ask Abel after his brother killed him. Ask Joseph after his brothers threw him in the pit (see Genesis 37:24). Ask Jesus, who was handed over to His persecutors because of envy (see Matthew 27:18). People who envy find fault with everyone. It's a spirit of universal censorship, like woke cancel culture. No one can please them, and everyone suffers because of them. They destroy more souls by their rules. In contrast, Adam Clark described the heart that does *not* envy as "ever willing that others should be preferred before them."

"Love does not parade itself, is not puffed up." Love is not a showoff. Don't do things just so others can see you, and don't try to be a people pleaser. Pride is one of the worst spiritual sins. You can smell it. It's obnoxious and arrogant. Don't let your head swell. Focus on the needs of others.

"Love … does not behave rudely." Those who lash out at others are not operating out of love. Love has good manners.

"Love … does not seek its own." Love is not cliquish. In Romans 12:10 Paul said, **"in honor giving preference to one another."** In Philippians 2:4 he said, **"Let each of you look out not only for his own interests, but also for the interests of others."** This is being like Jesus in the most basic, elemental way.

"Love … is not provoked." Love is not quick-tempered. Moses could not enter the promised land because he was provoked by the people's behavior (see Numbers 20:2-11).

"Love … thinks no evil." Love is not suspicious. It does not store up memories of wrongs received. It discards the hurts of the past instead of clinging to them. Real love doesn't suspect good actions are done with bad motives. When love believes in someone, it does not consider wrongs done and then forever evaluate the person according to their wrongdoing.

"Love … does not rejoice in iniquity, but rejoices in the truth." Love is not happy with evil.

FOUR MORE THINGS LOVE DOES

"Love bears all things, believes all things, hopes all things, endures all things." Charles Spurgeon, the Prince of Preachers, called these "love's four sweet companions"—strong, believing, hopeful, and enduring. We must have fervent charity for one another.

"Love bears all things." *All* means all, and translated literally this means, "love covers all things." 1 Peter 4:8 says, **"Love covers a multitude of sins."**

"Love ... believes all things." Choose to believe the best in others and hope for the best instead of the worst.

"Love ... hopes all things." Love is confident, not pessimistic, or negative. If our faith and hope in people has diminished because of something that happened, God can heal that.

"Love ... endures all things." This speaks for itself.

Here's the meat of the message:

"Love never fails. But whether there are prophecies, they will fail; whether there are tongues, they will cease; whether there is knowledge, it will vanish away. For we know in part and we prophesy in part. But when that which is perfect has come, then that which is in part will be done away."

"THAT WHICH IS PERFECT"

What does "that which is perfect" mean? Cessationists say the canonization of Scripture did away with tongues and prophecy. They have ceased. The problem with that interpretation is "knowledge" should also have vanished away.

Some say, "that which is perfect" refers to the second coming of Jesus. The implication is that all spiritual gifts will be done away with when Jesus comes. However, Jesus is not a "that." If He was, then why not just say, "when Jesus comes"? Also, the second coming will only bring a fullness of things we only partially experience now. Things will increase, not pass away. However, 1 Corinthians 13 never mentions the second coming of Christ or the end times.

The Scriptures are clear: the greatest outpouring of the Holy Spirit will come just prior to and during the millennial reign. I believe there will be a company of people who are so perfected in their faith that they will move in supernatural power just prior to and during the millennial reign. I believe there will be a remnant in the church who will reflect Joel 2 and will accomplish and do great supernatural feats.

The whole earth will be filled with the glory of God (see Psalm 72:19). There will be leaves for the healing of the nations and much more (see Revelation 22:2). Healing will continue to expand. Ezekiel speaks of God putting His Spirit in Israel and bringing them back to life (see Ezekiel 37:5). The fullness of the glory of the Lord will cover the earth. The supernatural will not decrease but increase, and not just for the millennium.

The last verse of 1 Corinthians 12 says, **"But earnestly desire the best gifts. And yet I show you a more excellent way."** Paul was essentially saying, "While we're discussing spiritual gifts, let me tell you how this all works. Let me show you a more excellent way. You can have all the gifts, but they must come from love." Then Paul spent all of chapter 13 explaining what *is* perfect. He said, **"Love never fails."**

Love makes the gifts more than just speaking. The spiritual gifts do not fulfill their potential without love. They become a "tinkling brass." Unfortunately, much of the tongue-speaking in the Pentecostal and Charismatic world is just noise that must be perfected in love. Isn't it interesting how some people with great spiritual gifts are rude and arrogant?

Speaking in tongues may be a manifestation of the Holy Spirit, but love is the fruit and evidence of the Holy Spirit. Even demons can prophesy. Shamans can heal the sick. The fruit of the Spirit is the evidence of the Holy Spirit far more than the gifts. **"By this all will know that you are My disciples, if you have love for one another" (John 13:35).**

When a believer ceases to be perfected in love, their speaking in tongues and prophecies will fall to the ground and become ineffective. Spiritual gifts without love cause an "in part" result that causes gifts to fail and words of knowledge to vanish.

Some believers have stopped growing and maturing in the Lord, but we must **"go on to perfection"** (see Hebrews 6:1) or the gifts will cease or diminish. **"We must grow up in all things into Him"** (see Ephesians 4:15). **"When I was a child, I spoke as a child, I understood as a child."** Paul is speaking of growing and maturing here. When we **"come to the measure of the stature of the fullness of Christ"** (see Ephesians 4:14), we will put away childish things.

The greatest hindrance to enhancing the spiritual gifts of tongues, prophecy, and spiritual knowledge is Christians being unperfected by God's love. Here are some verses that confirm the power of God's love: 1 John 4:18, **"Perfect love casts out fear."** Ephesians 3:19 says, **"to know the love of Christ which passes knowledge; that you may be filled with all the fullness of God."** Colossians 3:14, **"But above all these things put on love, which is the bond of perfection."**

Ephesians 4:15-16 says, **"but, speaking the truth in love, [we] may grow up in all things into Him who is the head—Christ—from whom the whole body, joined and knit together by what every joint supplies, according to the effective working by which every part does its share, causes growth of the body for the edifying of itself in love."**

Everything is tied to love. We can walk right now in the supernatural love of Christ.

"Father, my heart's desire for the prophetic community is that we grow up into all things in You. We don't want our tongues to cease. We don't want our prophecies to fall to the ground. We don't want our knowledge to vanish. We don't want to be a sounding brass or a tinkling cymbal. We want to be made perfect and complete in Your love and not just 'in part.' We want 'that which is perfect.' I pray for a fresh baptism of the full love of God to bring us into a full maturity of our gifts, full development of the prophetic, full development of prophecy and tongues, full discernment, and all the gifts of the Spirit.

"Lord, I believe when we exhibit Your character, You will trust us with Your power. The fullness of Your power is tied to the fullness of Your character. That is the only thing hindering or holding back more of the supernatural. We must be perfected in the love of God, which passes knowledge.

"Come, Holy Spirit, with a fresh baptism of love. Your Word says You shed abroad Your love in our hearts by the Holy Spirit which is given to us. I am asking for a company of people who will grow up in You to have a fresh baptism of Your love, so we can walk in all that You have for us in Jesus' name. May 'that which is perfect' come!

"Lord, I repent before You of any area of falling short of the glory of God. I repent before You of my sins and imperfections. I ask for a fresh grace. May the love of God bring us to completion, so we are not believers in a fallen world only believing 'in part' and frustrated. We want all that You have for us."

JACOB'S LADDER

In Jacob's journey with the Lord in Genesis 28, Jacob laid his head on some stones and began to dream. In his dream, he saw angels ascending and descending on a ladder that reached to heaven. He named that place *Bethel,* which means "house of God." Ladders are tools that enable us to reach higher levels than we can reach on our own. Climbing ladders can take us to new heights. They can also help us carry things from one level to another. On this particular ladder, the angels were bringing things from heaven to earth and from earth back to heaven.

At Bethel, there is a ladder that connects the earthly realm to the heavenly realm. God has made a way for us to access this heavenly realm and for the heavenly realm to have greater access to the earthly realm. This is *why* we can have angelic experiences, healings, and visions. God has always had a ladder that connects the earthly and heavenly realms, though sin often separates man from God.

In John 1:51, Jesus knew His listeners understood this Genesis 28 narrative. He demonstrated this when he shared his vision and prophetic word of knowledge with Philip and Nathanael, who were close friends. Philip believed Jesus was the Messiah, but Nathanael did not yet believe. After Jesus shared his vision of Nathanael sitting under a fig tree before they met, Nathanael finally believed. Jesus responded:

> **"Because I said to you, 'I saw you under the fig tree,' do you believe? You will see greater things than these." And He said to him, "Most assuredly, I say to you, hereafter you shall see heaven open, and the angels of God ascending and descending upon the Son of Man" (see John 1:50-51).**

Whenever Jesus demonstrated healing, deliverance, prophecy, visions, raising the dead, casting out demons, or cleansing lepers, heaven came down on Him, through this ladder, and manifested the kingdom of God through Him to give us all a taste of heaven. When Jesus said to Nathanael, **"You shall see ... the angels of God ascending and descending on the Son of Man,"** He knew their minds would immediately think back to their cherished patriarch, Jacob, and Genesis 28. He was setting the stage for them.

Science tells us our human DNA looks like a spiraling ladder with individual strands in steps. Within our human DNA is the ability to climb spiritual ladders—to climb higher in reality, consciousness, experience, and power, one step at a time.

With this ladder also ascending and descending on Jesus, we cannot separate Jesus' power from His DNA and character. Supernatural activity *without* God's character is witchcraft. That is not to say that every person the Lord uses must have perfect character. We all go through a process of sanctification, but the Lord wants us to have *His* character. There are nine fruit and nine gifts of the Spirit. The character of Jesus is embodied in the fruit. Jesus said, **"He who abides in Me, and I in him, bears much fruit."** However, if we are *not* fruitful, we will be cut off from the vine (see John 15:5-6).

We must have the fruit of the Spirit to balance out the gifts of the Spirit. Some of the most dangerous people in church history who committed terrible atrocities were those who had gifts without fruit. For example, Jim Jones, the infamous American cult leader, was a very gifted preacher at one time. However, his character did not increase with his gifts, and he ended up committing the mass murder of his cult members. So, what good is the gift of prophecy without the fruit of meekness? All we do is brag and talk about how great we are. Character must increase with the gifts.

We must be challenged to climb higher on Jacob's ladder and bring the heavenly to the earthly realm and the earthly to the heavenly realm. We must have the fruit of the Spirit to *keep* us where the gifts of the Spirit *take* us. So, what are the steps of this ladder? I believe they are found in one of the most oft-quoted passages in Scripture—the Beatitudes.

THE BEATITUDES LADDER

Blessed are the poor in spirit, for theirs is the kingdom of heaven. Blessed are those who mourn, for they shall be comforted. Blessed are the meek, for they shall inherit the earth. Blessed are those who hunger and thirst for righteousness, for they shall be filled. Blessed are the merciful, for they shall obtain mercy. Blessed are the pure in heart, for they shall see God. Blessed are the peacemakers, for they shall be called sons of God. Blessed are those who are persecuted for righteousness' sake, for theirs is the kingdom of heaven.

Blessed are you when they revile and persecute you, and say all kinds of evil against you falsely for My sake. Rejoice and be exceedingly glad, for great is your reward in heaven, for so they persecuted the prophets who were before you (Matthew 5:3-12).

Here Jesus connected our progression in His character and likeness to man's heavenly image when we were first created, before we were marred by sin and fell "off the ladder." After the fall, our years were shortened, and our quality of life diminished. Jesus also connected the Beatitudes to the prophets and to persecution, which is often associated with true prophetic ministry. Understanding and getting heaven's perspective on the prophetic requires us spending time in the heavenly realms. Being made in His image and likeness also helps God trust us with more revelation.

In the Beatitudes, Jesus established both the nature and aspirations for the citizens of His kingdom. We both have and are learning these character traits. Each Beatitude or character trait reflects Christ's image and represents various marks and goals for all believers.

Acts 10:38 says, **"How God anointed Jesus of Nazareth with the Holy Spirit and with power, who went about doing good and healing all who were oppressed by the devil, for God was with Him."** Jesus went about doing good *and* healing. He had the character *and* the gifts in that order. The more we develop the nature and character of Jesus, the more we are entrusted with Jesus' power. Many people chase the gifts without the character, but the fruit come before the gifts. Ladders work one step at a time. We cannot major in one trait to the exclusion of the others. We all have areas that need strengthening.

Not coincidentally, the last word of the last chapter of the last book of the Old Testament is "curse." In contrast, the opening sermon of our Lord's ministry in the New Testament begins with "blessed." Jesus said, "Blessed are." This is present tense. Charles Spurgeon said, "Note, also with delight that the blessing is in every case in the present tense, a happiness to be now enjoyed and delighted in." Jesus did not say, "blessed you shall be." *Blessed* means "happy." "Blessed are the poor in spirit" means internal blessings. Blessed also means a joy within that no circumstances can change. The Greek word translated *blessed* means "a joy that chance or change cannot stop."

Step #1: "Blessed are the poor in spirit, for theirs is the kingdom of God."

This is not a human confession of self-deprivation or self-hatred. We are not by nature insignificant or personally without value. Instead, this is a confession that man is sinful, rebellious, and utterly without moral virtue adequate to justify himself to God. In ourselves, we are utterly and morally bankrupt.

We recognize that we cannot buy anything from God, including salvation. We have nothing to offer God. We recognize our moral virtues are inadequate. We have no spiritual assets. If we break one commandment, we break them all. We cannot be 98% keepers of the law. We know we can never offer God anything that will impress Him. The ancient Greeks had different words for the "working poor" and the "truly poor." Jesus used the word "truly poor" here. It literally means one who must beg for everything they have.

"Poverty of spirit" can also be a pseudo poverty of spirit, which can be artificially induced by false humility. People with false humility will make self-deprecating comments like, "I don't really deserve this," when deep down they think the opposite. They are proud. Likewise, a pseudo poverty of spirit can be artificially induced by self-hatred. Only the Holy Spirit and our response to His working in us can bring about true poverty of spirit. Only by grace. We cannot do enough good to earn it. Many seeker-friendly churches refuse to talk about this. They'll say, "God loves us just the way we are, whether we ever change or not." True humility recognizes that, within ourselves we have a sinful nature with which to contend. It is **not of works, lest anyone should boast" (see Ephesians 2:9).** We are saved by "nothing but the blood of Jesus."

This beatitude comes first, because this is where we all must begin with God. Charles Spurgeon said:

"A ladder, if it is to be of any use, must have its first step near the ground, or feeble climbers will never be able to mount. It would have been a grievous discouragement to struggling faith if the first blessing had been given to the pure in heart; to that excellence the young beginner makes no claim, while to poverty of spirit he can reach without going beyond his line. Everyone can start here; it isn't first blessed are the pure or the holy or the spiritual or the wonderful. Everyone can be poor in spirit. "Not what I have, but what I have not, is the first point of contact between my soul and God."

We cannot take credit for anything. Left to ourselves, we are spiritually bankrupt. Pride comes before a fall (see Proverbs 16:18), and we don't want to fall off the ladder. The times when I have failed the Lord began when I was feeling confident in my own strength and ability.

"Blessed are the poor in spirit, for theirs is the kingdom of heaven." What is the kingdom of heaven? It is all the gifts, all prophetic revelation, and all of heaven coming down the ladder. The kingdom of heaven is not based on race, merit, zeal, or wealth. Instead, it is given to the poor, the despised, the prostitutes, and those who have nothing to offer God, so they do not try. Instead, they cry for mercy and are heard.

The thief on the cross had nothing to offer. He simply asked Jesus to remember him when He entered paradise. James and John argued over who would sit at Jesus' right and left hand, but when Jesus entered His kingdom, to His right and left were two thieves with nothing to offer. A popular Eastern Orthodox prayer says, "Lord Jesus Christ, Son of God, have mercy on me, a sinner."

The call to be "poor in spirit" comes first because it puts all the proceeding commands in perspective. None can be fulfilled in our own strength, only through our reliance on God's power. No one mourns, no one is meek, no one hungers for righteousness, no one is merciful, no one is pure in heart, no one is prophetic, until they are first poor in spirit.

We cannot skip any steps on this ladder. Some people say, "Give me dreams; let me see angels and future events and prophesy about them." But are you a peacemaker? Is your heart pure? How merciful are you? How much do you hunger and thirst for righteousness? How meek are you? How much do you mourn? Are you poor in spirit? We all must start at the bottom of the ladder and work our way up. The closer we get to the top of the ladder, the closer we get to the heavenly realms, because the ladder connects heaven with earth. But it all begins with the first step.

Step #2: "Blessed are those who mourn, for they shall be comforted."

The Greek grammar here indicates an intense degree of mourning. Jesus is not speaking of casual sorrow for the consequences of our sin and evil but a deep grieving before God over our fallen state. The "mourning" is for us and for the low and needy condition of others in our society. Those who mourn for their sins and sinful condition are promised comfort. 2 Corinthians 7:10 says, **"For godly sorrow produces repentance leading to salvation, not to be regretted; but the sorrow of the world produces death."** God allows grieving and mourning in our lives as a path, not a destination.

Mourning allows us to know something special about God, the fellowship of His sufferings, and a closeness to Jesus. Philippians 3:10 says, **"that I may know Him and the power of His resurrection, and the fellowship of His sufferings, being conformed to His death, if, by any means, I may attain to the resurrection from the dead."** Isaiah 53:3 describes Jesus as, **"a Man of sorrows and acquainted with grief."**

Much of modern psychology and seeker-friendly Christianity try to provide an excuse and escape from the grief of our sins. Freudian psychology blames parents and others. We cannot mourn until we realize just how poor in spirit we are. If we fall off this ladder, we can get back on it. After we realize how morally and spiritually bankrupt we are, we can mourn and be comforted, but we cannot stay there.

Step #3: "Blessed are the meek, for they shall inherit the earth."

It is impossible to translate this ancient Greek word *praus*, translated here "meekness," into one English word. It is the perfect balance between anger and indifference; it is a powerful personality properly controlled and humble. Meekness is not weakness but strength under control, like a stallion that has been broken. It is suffering a wrong without bitterness or desire to avenge or retaliate. We give others too much control over our emotions.

The first two beatitudes are mostly inward. The third step on the ladder, meekness, deals more with how we relate to others. The first two are mainly negative; the third is clearly positive. When we live in the first two beatitudes, it is difficult to be proud and arrogant. Those who skip the first two steps will have a hard time being meek. We climbed on the ladder because we realized how spiritually bankrupt we were. This led us to mourn for ourselves and for others, then look at others with meekness.

Only carnal people think meekness is weakness. Meekness means a willingness to submit and work under proper authority, while disregarding our own rights and privileges. **"Nevertheless not My will, but Yours, be done" (see Luke 22:42).**

It is one thing for us to admit to our own spiritual bankruptcy, but what happens when someone else does that for us? What if someone calls us a racist or bigot? Do we react meekly? The blessed demonstrate meekness in the face of evil and injustice. Unfortunately, prophetic people can be more prideful than any other faction in the church. "Who prophesied this first?" "Who had the first word?"

The meek will control their desire for their rights and privileges because they are confident God will watch over and protect them. This promise, **"Blessed are the meek, for they shall inherit the earth,"** proves that God will not allow His meek ones to get the short end of the stick. Justice eventually comes for all. Gifted people sometimes hurt each other. How do we respond? The earth was created for the sons of men. Once we step through the first three blessings, we can inherit all the promises God has for us.

By the time we reach the third step, we realize that our natural man finds no happiness or blessedness in spiritual poverty, mourning, or meekness. These are only blessings for our spirit man, created in Christ Jesus. Sometimes we can get so caught up in monitoring the carnal behavior of others that we lose focus on our own spirituality. The Beatitudes are spiritual blessings for spiritual people.

If we don't preach a gospel of going through the first three steps, we should not expect a congregation that hungers and thirsts for righteousness. We must preach against sin and speak of our need for a Savior. If we want reformation, we must first preach repentance, which calls both saints and sinners to repentance. The altar is also for the saint. The more hyper grace we preach in Western Christianity, the more carnal and lukewarm the church becomes.

Step #4: "Blessed are those who hunger and thirst for righteousness, for they shall be filled."

This gift from God that grants us the desire to hunger and thirst for righteousness comes after we receive the first three blessings. We can tell how hungry a person is by how they eat. Many pastors who have tried to force-feed the meat and potatoes of righteousness to their congregations have discovered they would rather eat the cotton candy of easy believing and self-help.

This verse refers to the *condition* of righteousness or the condition of our lives, not positional righteousness. When we repented, God treated us as if we had never sinned. That is our positional righteousness in Him. However, when it comes to our condition, we must still work things out through sanctification (see Philippians 2:12). These are the nuts and bolts of Christianity, which have *everything* to do with the prophetic. We cannot jump to step eight.

Spiritual hunger is a gift from God; we want God. It's just as real as physical hunger and thirst, except this hunger can be more intense and painful, like physical hunger pains. Spiritual hunger can become a driving force, just like natural hunger can drive us to great lengths. Spiritual hunger is also a sign of health, just like natural hunger is a sign of health.

We see Christians and prophetic people hunger for many things—fame, success, power, authority, comfort, happiness—but how many of them hunger and thirst for righteousness? Jesus said this to a culture that truly understood how it felt to be hungry and thirsty. It is more difficult for our Western culture to understand this.

Charles Spurgeon wrote, "'Alas!' says he, 'It is not enough for me to know that my sin is forgiven. I have a fountain of sin within my heart, and bitter waters continually flow from it. Oh, that my nature could be changed, so that I, the lover of sin, could be made a lover of that which is good; that I, now full of evil, could become full of holiness?'" *That* is spiritual hunger.

Step #5: "Blessed are the merciful, for they shall obtain mercy."

This beatitude speaks to those who have already received God's mercy. It is mercy to be emptied of pride and arrogance and brought to poverty of spirit. It is mercy to be brought to mourning over our spiritual condition. It is mercy to receive meekness and become gentle. It is mercy to be made hungry and thirsty for righteousness. So, those who are expected to *show* mercy have already *received* God's mercy.

However, if we want to receive mercy from others *including* God, we need to be merciful to others. Those who often best show mercy are the ones who started at the bottom of the ladder. They realized four steps ago how much they needed mercy.

David was merciful to Saul even when Saul was trying to kill him. This is one reason God showed mercy to David when he sinned. In David, the merciful obtained mercy. In 1 Kings 1 when Saul died and someone came to tell David about Saul's death, David had the messenger put to death because he touched God's anointed. David even invited Mephibosheth, Saul's grandson, to sit at his table after David became king. Blessed are the merciful, for they shall obtain mercy. To whom is God calling you to be merciful? If you are not merciful, you may have to go back to step one and start reclimbing.

Step #6: "Blessed are the pure in heart, for they shall see God."

In the Greek language, "pure in heart" carries with it the connotation of straightness, honesty, and clarity. Two connotations are connected to this: One is moral purity as opposed to ceremonial purity; the other is a single, undivided heart. It speaks of those who are utterly sincere and undivided in their devotion and commitment to God. They may have faults, but they go after God 100%. "Pure in heart" is the opposite of doublemindedness.

"The pure in heart" are not just pure in language and actions. Jesus addressed our inward condition, not just our outward behavioral modification. He said if we just look at a woman to lust after her, we have already committed adultery with her in our hearts (see Matthew 5:28). Likewise, if we have hate in our hearts, we have already committed murder. Many people put on a good act; they dress holy but hide lust in their hearts.

We also often criticize in others what we overlook in ourselves. I did this in my own life. I was angry at someone but then realized I had jealousy in my own heart. **"Who may ascend into the hill of the Lord? Or who may stand in His holy place? He who has clean hands and a pure heart"** (see Psalm 24:3-4). We must clean our hearts, motives, and behaviors. The nature of Christ has everything to do with the power of Christ.

The pure in heart receive the most wonderful reward: **"they shall see God."** Our spiritual perceptions are opened, we enjoy greater intimacy with God, and He can reveal Himself, His will, and the secrets of men's hearts to us. The polluting sins of covetousness, oppression, lust, and deception have a definite blinding effect on our spiritual perceptions. The pure in heart are freed from these pollutions. We can see God in nature, in Scripture, and in His church family. This intimate relationship with God must become our greatest motivation for purity, greater than even the fear of being caught or its consequences. To be pure in heart is to have the character of Christ. The loudest voices in heaven are human thoughts. Have you ever thought, "Thank God no one knows what I just thought?" Heaven's perception of things is quite different from ours.

Step #7: "Blessed are the peacemakers, for they shall be called sons of God."

This verse does not refer to those who have or live in peace but to those who bring or *make* peace. They overcome evil with good (see Romans 12:21). One way we do this is by spreading the gospel, since God has entrusted to us the ministry of reconciliation (see 2 Corinthians 5:18). Instead of taking sides in an argument or determining who's right and wrong, we become the healing balm. James 3:17 says, **"But the wisdom that is from above is first pure, then peaceable."** Notice godly wisdom is first pure, then peaceable. We are first pure in heart, then we become peacemakers. These are all steps we must climb on the ladder.

Step #8: "Blessed are those who are persecuted for righteousness' sake, for theirs is the kingdom of heaven. ... For so they persecuted the prophets who were before you."

The blessed are persecuted for righteousness' sake and for Jesus' sake, not for the sake of their stupid choices and fanaticisms. **"For so they persecuted the prophets."** Peter recognized that suffering could also come to Christians for reasons other than faithfulness to Jesus. 1 Peter 4:15-16: **"But let none of you suffer as a murderer, a thief, an evildoer, or as a busybody in other people's matters. Yet if anyone suffers as a Christian, let him not be ashamed, but let him glorify God in this matter."**

This final step identifies us with the prophets. We might even be thrown in the lion's den. God can entrust us with more when we take things one step at a time. The last step on the ladder is persecution for righteousness' sake, **"For so they persecuted the prophets."** When we reach the last step in the heavenly realm, we are identified with the prophets.

DISCUSSION QUESTIONS

1. Why do you think 1 Corinthians 13, the great love chapter, is placed between 1 Corinthians 12 and 14, talking about the gifts of the Holy Spirit? Explain.

2. In your own words, define *agape*. How does *agape* differ from the other Greek words for love: *phileo, storge,* and *eros*?

3. Of the fourteen definitions for love Paul provided in 1 Corinthians 13, which one stands out to you the most and why?

4. Since Paul taught that "love never fails," and since anything that never fails is perfect, Paul could be saying "that which is perfect" in 1 Corinthians 13:10 is love. Can you think of some other reasons this might be true?

5. What is the purpose of Jacob's ladder in Genesis 28 and John 1? Explain.

6. What is the connection between Jacob's ladder and the Beatitudes? Explain.

7. In your own words, what does it mean to be "poor in spirit"? Why is this the first and most important beatitude and step on Jacob's ladder?

8. Thinking of the Beatitudes in terms of steps on a ladder, where do you currently see yourself on this ladder? What steps do you feel you have already conquered and what steps do you feel you have yet to conquer? Explain.

9. Why is understanding and practicing the "Beatitudes Ladder" so important to operating in the prophetic? Explain.

"The empowering anointing comes once we find our purposes and accept our assignments."

POWER IN
the Prophetic

The most important key to learning how to function in a prophetic anointing is believing that it can happen through us.

There are diversities of gifts, but the same Spirit. There are differences of ministries, but the same Lord. And there are diversities of activities, but it is the same God who works all in all. But the manifestation of the Spirit is given to each one for the profit of all: for to one is given the word of wisdom through the Spirit, to another the word of knowledge through the same Spirit, to another faith by the same Spirit, to another gifts of healings by the same Spirit, to another the working of miracles, to another prophecy, to another discerning of spirits, to another different kinds of tongues, to another the interpretation of tongues. But one and the same Spirit works all these things, distributing to each one individually as He wills. (1 Corinthians 12:4-11).

"The Spirit of the Lord is upon Me, because He has anointed Me to preach the gospel to the poor; He has sent Me to heal the brokenhearted, to proclaim liberty to the captives and recovery of sight to the blind, to set at liberty those who are oppressed; to proclaim the acceptable year of the Lord" (Luke 4:18).

It shall come to pass in that day that his burden will be taken away from your shoulder, and his yoke from your

neck, and the yoke will be destroyed <u>because of the</u> <u>anointing</u> oil. (Isaiah 10:27).

DON'T TRADE YOUR ANOINTING

Anointings are tangible. We want the intangible to become tangible, the invisible to become visible, and the inaudible to become audible. We determine how far anointings can go. When we overcome temptation, anointings can go farther.

Esau was born first, while Jacob, the supplanter and trickster, kept reaching for Esau's heel. Jacob was on the heels of a blessing. Esau was always just ahead of Jacob. Yet, Esau did not recognize the value of this birthright anointing. It cost him nothing. When we receive something by entitlement, it doesn't mean as much to us, so we tend to take it for granted. This birthright anointing had been sitting idle in Esau's life, so he traded his birthright anointing for a bowl of soup. He did not understand its eternal value. In a moment of vulnerability, his flesh gave up his birthright. He could easily have gone to the house and eaten. He did not understand the great cost of trading spiritual things for physical things, like anointings and birthrights for soup.

Jacob, on the other hand, understood and appreciated the birthright. He was happy to give up the physical for the spiritual. Never trade your anointing for something carnal. Satan loves to take advantage of the Esau types of this world. He is more aware than most of the power of that anointing.

Jesus performed no recorded miracle until he was thirty, yet He always possessed an anointing. If Jesus had performed miracles as God and not man, we would feel disqualified. He performed every miracle as a man who overcame temptation and human nature like we do. Jesus did not use His anointing to consume it on His own lusts. He did not turn stones into bread when He was fasting, as Satan suggested. The anointing is not to serve us but to serve others. The anointing you already possess will be released when you value that anointing more than carnal, natural things.

The patriarchs of the faith were Abraham, Isaac, and Jacob, not Esau. Though Jacob had character flaws, he desired the anointing more than temporal things. Jesus also recognized the value of His anointing and was unwilling to give it up when tempted. We may not fully understand the value of our anointings, but our enemy sure does. People who are unsure of their identity in Christ are more easily tricked by the enemy because they also don't know what anointings they carry.

After Jesus was baptized, the Father said, **"This is My beloved son, in whom I am well pleased"** (see Matthew 3:17). The devil's first words when he came to tempt Jesus were, **"If you are the Son of God"** (see Matthew 4:3). He wanted Jesus to question who He was, just as he wanted Eve to question what God said, **"Has God indeed said?"** (see Genesis 3:1).

HOW ANOINTINGS WORK

If you want to know the future, know the past. Our anointings take on whatever we did in the past or as a child—our interests, desires, and strengths. This helps create our prophetic filter. Moses was meek and became a spokesperson. Joshua was by nature a fighter and led the fight into the promised land. Our faith and fingerprints are unique. We should not compare ourselves to others. God likes originals.

When Saul of Tarsus met Ananias, who was prophetic, he laid hands on Saul, and Saul became apostolic. God designs each of us uniquely, so our anointings complement who we are. Peter, a fisherman, became a fisher of men. The Lord instructed him to let down his nets to increase his capacity. Peter cast down one net, and his net broke. Our anointings will bring us more than we can retain. After Peter spoke on the day of Pentecost, 3,000 came into the kingdom. God anoints us to carry only what we can carry. Still, we should not limit the capacity for what God can do through us.

A person who is deaf and mute can never be possessed by a spirit of gossip. Spirits can only work through what we already are or through the strengths we already possess. The spirit world takes advantage of the strengths we already have. Artistic people can easily be prophetic because pictures are already familiar to them. Moses was put down in the water and taken by Pharoah's daughter. The first thing we learn about Moses is that he came by water, so why should we be surprised that nearly all his miracles involved water? His first miracle involved turning water into blood, then parting the Red Sea, then making bitter water sweet, then striking water from a rock. His past reflected his future, which was unique to him.

If you loved playing with G.I. Joe action figures when you were a kid, maybe you will operate in spiritual warfare. I liked flying, Superman, and planes. I often dreamed I was flying. What we did or desired in the past is prophetic regarding our future anointings. Philippians 2:13 says, **"for it is God who works in you both to will and to do for His good pleasure."** God wills and does His good pleasure through us. Our past interest in books and history may set us up for future government work or something similar.

Esau lost his birthright because it wasn't valuable to him. The enemy will always try to steal what is valuable. Whatever may be coming under attack in our lives right now is probably tied to our future purposes in God. Former drug addicts become counselors.

If you grew up, like I did, with regular nightmares, you may be called to be a dreamer, like Joseph. The enemy loves to keep us from dreaming by frightening us with nightmares. Joseph was a dreamer. It nearly killed him, but then it became his calling to interpret dreams. The enemy will always attack the hardest where our anointings lie. The enemy will try to take out naturally gifted leaders in their youth to keep them from operating in their anointings later.

One major key to knowing our anointings is what we desire. If we are drawn to the medical field, that could be us trying to fulfill in the natural our spiritual calling to heal. The nine gifts of the Spirit work differently for everyone. There are also nine fruits of the Spirit to control and protect those gifts, so we don't become prideful. Our anointings come to fit us for our callings and have unique fingerprints. Let them make you the best you!

HOW TO INCREASE OUR ANOINTINGS

The prophet Elijah told a woman needing food to gather vessels, but not just a few vessels (see 2 Kings 4:3). When all the vessels were filled, the oil stopped flowing. The extent of our anointings is determined by our ability to increase our capacities. How many more vessels might this woman have brought and been even more blessed? Are we willing to increase our Bible reading and prayer time to increase our anointing capacity?

Impartations make poor substitutes for what we have available to us through the Holy Spirit. Impartations come from human spirits, like how Elisha received a double portion of Elijah's spirit. However, we already have much more imparted by the Holy Spirit. If you want to walk in your anointing, detangle your life, so there's less of you and more of God. God's supply is larger than our capacity to retain it. Ephesians 3:20-21: **"Now to Him who**

is able to do exceedingly abundantly above all that we ask or think, <u>according to the power that works in us</u>, to Him be glory in the church by Christ Jesus to all generations, forever and ever." Our anointings come according to the power that works in us. How many vessels did we gather? How many nets did we let down? We determine how far we can go with God.

I started ministering at the age of fourteen. I felt called at age twelve with limited understanding. I began cleaning toilets in the youth area. In the first church I pastored, at age twenty-five, I had to use buckets to catch leaking rainwater from ruining the pews. The church was $100,000 in debt, had only three givers, and a new roof was needed. Yet all three problems were resolved in three years. The Lord stretched my abilities and increased my capacity to see, even at a young age.

If we want to advance our anointings and be used by God in big ways, we must increase our capacity. We put such high demands on God yet such little demands on ourselves. If you normally read a book a month, read two. If you can play one musical instrument, learn another. The water of the Spirit takes the shape of whatever vessel it fills. The same anointing that caused Moses to stretch the rod and part the Red Sea was the same anointing that caused Joshua to part the Jordan by stepping into it. They were different people using different methods, but they both worked under the same anointing.

We prophesy by our anointings, yet there are different kinds of anointings. We need to understand how these anointings work, which anointing we are cooperating with, and the different purposes behind those anointings. Seeing things from a biblical perspective will really help us in the prophetic and supernatural. The various levels and administrations of the prophetic work by anointings.

THE ABIDING ANOINTING

"But <u>the anointing which you have received of Him abides in you</u>, and you do not need that anyone teach you; but as the same anointing teaches you concerning all things, and is true, and is not a lie, and just as it has taught you, you will abide in Him" (1 John 2:27).

The abiding anointing is for every believer, and it is *not* the least important anointing. In fact, it is our foundational and fundamental anointing. If we do not maintain this anointing, this anointing cannot maintain us. It is an anointing for living. Based on what John said, it is an anointing within that deepens and sustains our fellowship with God. It is the anointing we receive when we receive the Holy Spirit. It is for living, not doing.

The abiding anointing is not for our purpose or our ministry. It is for growing in our personal encounters with the Lord, because the Holy Spirit abides in us. We wait daily on the Lord, spending time in His Word. We stir up this anointing that is in us. This abiding anointing enables us to bear fruit. Jesus said, **"He who abides in Me, and I in Him, bears much fruit"** (see John 15:5). God's number one priority is not for us to receive great prophetic words or even to build great churches, but for us to maintain our walk with Him. This anointing comes from no man and cannot be imparted. This anointing is from the Lord.

This anointing is for our spirit, not for our soul, mind, will, emotions, or body. This anointing provides grace to stay in the things of God. It is for our spiritual development. We can have this anointing and still have illnesses and other things in our bodies. It is not an anointing for big meetings, prophecy, healing the sick, or for fivefold ministry.

However, this anointing must be the foundation of every believer. By this anointing, we develop, foster, and grow in personal fellowship and intimacy with the Lord. This anointing keeps us hungry for His Word and keeps us on the path of life. **"The path of the just is like the shining sun, that shines ever brighter unto the perfect day"** (see Proverbs 4:18). To stay on that path, we must maintain this anointing.

We must also value the abiding anointing as much or more than we value other anointings. In fact, no other anointing matters if we don't stir up this anointing in our lives. We must not neglect it. We set ourselves up for problems if we do not keep this anointing first and, instead, try to live off the other anointings, because this anointing is maintained by our fellowship with the Lord.

So, this first anointing is of Him. He is the source. It *is* Him. It is Him possessing us and us possessing Him. This anointing abides; it doesn't come and go. It is daily fellowship with the Lord. In the Old Testament, the Lord was referred to as "I AM" (see Exodus 3:14). He is the same yesterday, and today, and forever (see Hebrews 13:8). He is our healer, deliverer, way maker, husband, and friend. He is the most important in our lives. Make sure that it can be said at the end of your life that you "abided in Him." Other anointings may come and go, but His abiding anointing must remain. It is possible to maintain other anointings and lose Him.

This daily fellowship with the Lord is our most important priority. If you don't spend time with Him early, you'll feel like something is missing the entire day. Seek Him early, from the rising of the sun. Nurture fellowship with Him. When you start your day with the Lord, He'll bring a completeness to your day so, come hell or high water, you'll face nothing alone.

You cannot tend to this anointing once a week and expect to maintain it. You must keep it stirred. It gets stirred when we wait on the Lord, pray in the Spirit, and spend time fellowshipping with Him. If you don't maintain this, don't complain when you don't have dreams or visionary encounters, or when the Lord doesn't appear to you. This is not a legalistic thing but a relational thing. If you don't nurture this, you may feel like the Lord isn't moving in your life, and He hasn't moved, but you have. We cannot take this anointing for granted.

Without this anointing, we can end up hurting people, because this anointing develops and releases the fruit of the Spirit. It provides a peace and stability that we cannot manufacture or live without. Without this anointing, other anointings are just experiences.

This anointing teaches us and helps us to learn and to understand God. We can be in a "dead" church service, and the abiding anointing can still teach us, because the anointing in us helps us extrapolate things. We hear the Word within words, and this keeps us from lies and deceptions. This anointing protects us and keeps us abiding in truth. When we hear something that is unscriptural or false, we'll immediately recognize it, because it doesn't bear witness with our spirit. The Holy Spirit teacher in us helps us understand.

The Holy Spirit teaches us all things. He helps us understand His Word and messages from others. 1 John 2:27 says, **"this anointing teaches you concerning all things, and is true, and not a lie."** We'll know what is true and what is a lie. It helps us discern without suspicion and protects us and keeps us in truth like a safety net.

THE EMPOWERING ANOINTING

The empowering anointing is for service, for our callings and ministries, and for being witnesses to the Lord. If we are anointed to speak or write, this anointing empowers us to do those things.

"But you shall receive power when the Holy Spirit has come upon you; and you shall be witnesses to Me both in Jerusalem, and in all Judea and Samaria, and to the end of the earth" (Acts 1:8). Here in Acts 1, Jesus told His disciples to go to Jerusalem and wait. All they wanted to know was if He was going to restore the kingdom back to Israel. They still wanted Him to be their political messiah. He said it was not for them to know the times or seasons which the Father had put in His own power. **"But you shall receive power when the Holy Spirit has come upon you" (Acts 1:8).**

Here we progress from the anointing that abides "in us" to the anointing that comes "upon us" to be His witnesses. We go from being to doing. This empowering anointing comes once we find our purposes and acknowledge or accept our assignments. This anointing comes on us to minister, but when we're finished ministering, the anointing lifts off us. I can well relate to this.

I remember once when Paul Keith Davis ministered an important word at MorningStar. After he finished, he looked at me and asked if I had anything to add, but I didn't. There must be an agreement between the Word and the Spirit for us to minister. We need both. If you want the empowering anointing, find God's will and purpose for your life, then He will give you the grace and anointing to complete that gift or ministry He has given to you.

Years ago, Paul Cain and R.T. Kendall coauthored a book called *The Word and the Spirit: Reclaiming Your Covenant With the*

Holy Spirit and the Word of God. In it, R.T. wrote about the unique unification of the Word and the Spirit. He came from a non-charismatic background. However, after he met Mike Bickle and Rick Joyner, he realized that God was developing a unity between the Evangelical (Word) and Charismatic (Spirit) branches of the church.

I believe the Lord desires a bridal company to live out and express that unification of the Word of God and the Spirit of God. If we try to read the Word of God without the Spirit of God, it's nothing but black and red ink on white pages. If we have the Spirit of God without the Word of God, we can veer off into some pretty wacky stuff. There must be a unification of the Word and the Spirit.

Anointings come for a purpose or an assignment, and when we finish that purpose or assignment, the anointings lift. Jesus was born with the abiding anointing from the Father, but then the empowering anointing came *on* Him. **"For unto us a Child is born, unto us a Son is given; and the government will be upon His shoulder. And His name will be called Wonderful, Counselor, Mighty God, Everlasting Father, Prince of Peace"** **(Isaiah 9:6).**

After Jesus' baptism, a change happened. The Spirit descended and rested *on* Him, like a dove. Matthew 3:16 says: **"When He had been baptized, Jesus came up immediately from the water; and behold, the heavens were opened to Him, and He saw the Spirit of God descending like a dove and alighting upon Him."** From that point forward, miracles happened.

WE HAVE THE ABIDING ANOINTING IF...

It is possible to be deceived with the Spirit *upon* us, but it is not possible to be deceived with the Spirit working *in* us. The abiding anointing keeps us in truth and out of deception. That is why someone can be gifted to minister yet end up deceived. It's possible to be used by the Lord but no longer know the Lord. Matthew 7:22-23 says,

> **"Many will say to Me in that day, 'Lord, Lord, have we not prophesied in Your name, cast out demons in Your name, and done many wonders in Your name?' And then I will declare to them, 'I never knew you; depart from Me, you who practice lawlessness!'"**

Some of the most gifted people in church history have fallen into deception because they didn't stay in the abiding anointing while under the empowering anointing. Jim Jones was once an anointed preacher with many gifts of healings and words of knowledge, but then he gave into his flesh and destroyed many lives. He abandoned the abiding anointing. We can only keep the empowering anointing on us for so long once we start neglecting the abiding anointing.

Many people desire the empowering anointing for service (or attention) but neglect the abiding anointing. King Saul is an example of this. When Saul became king, the Bible says there was not a better person in all of Israel and he could prophesy with the prophets. He was meek and humble, recognized his humble beginnings coming from the least tribe, but then he received his empowering anointing and started neglecting his abiding anointing. He fell into deception and even consulted a witch because he could no longer hear from the Lord. Samson is another example of the Spirit coming upon someone to do great feats, but then he laid his head in the lap of a harlot.

Ephesians 3:20 says, **"Now to Him who is able to do exceedingly abundantly above all that we ask or think, according to the power that works in us"** This speaks of the abiding anointing *in* us for walking with the Lord. The empowering anointing is for working; the abiding anointing is for personal revelations and encounters. The Lord will share His secrets with those who walk in the abiding anointing. The empowering anointing is for demonstration.

How do we know if we have the abiding anointing? We have a hunger for the Lord. We read His Word and pray and meditate. We have a godly routine of waiting on the Lord. We have faith and expectation to receive from Him when we're sick or need provisions for our needs. We have faith that the Lord will use us to prophesy. We fellowship with the Lord, practice His presence, and hunger for prayer. We worship, intercede, and remain in union with Him.

WE HAVE AN EMPOWERING ANOINTING IF...

The empowering anointing makes the difference in ministry. It is a gift given. The empowering anointing is also transferable, while the abiding anointing is not. No one can transfer the abiding anointing or a hunger for the Lord.

1 Samuel 10:6-7 says, **"Then the Spirit of the Lord will come upon you, and you will prophesy with them and be turned into another man. And let it be, when these signs come to you, that you do as the occasion demands; for God is with you."**

We can "do as the occasion demands" when we have an empowering anointing, which can also be dangerous. Mishandling this empowering anointing and gift can get us killed. Just ask Uzzah. 2 Samuel 6:6-7 says,

"And when they came to Nachon's threshing floor, Uzzah put out his hand to the ark of God and took hold of it, for the oxen stumbled. Then the anger of the Lord was aroused

against Uzzah, and God struck him there for his error; and he died there by the ark of God."

How do we know if we have an empowering anointing? **"Praising God and having favor with all the people. And the Lord added to the church daily those who were being saved"** (Acts 2:47). We know we have an empowering anointing when the Lord adds to the church. **"Now in those days, when the number of the disciples was multiplying"** (Acts 6:1). We know we have an empowering anointing when the disciples multiply. **Then the word of God spread, and the number of the disciples multiplied greatly"** (Acts 6:7) We know we have an empowering anointing when the disciples *greatly* multiply. Growth and gathering are evidence of the empowering anointing.

Acts 19:11 says, **"Now God worked unusual miracles by the hands of Paul, so that even handkerchiefs or aprons were brought from his body to the sick, and the diseases left them and the evil spirits went out of them."** The empowering anointing can even be transferred through handkerchiefs. It is transferable and tangible.

The abiding anointing is for our spirits; the empowering anointing can affect our souls and bodies and even our weaknesses. It also magnifies everything, including our weaknesses. Samson and Elijah are examples of weaknesses being magnified under the empowering anointing. It can take us from our highest highs to our lowest lows. Samson killed a thousand Philistines with the jawbone of a donkey, then lay with Delilah and lost everything. Elijah called down fire from heaven and a few hours later was quaking in his boots for fear of Jezebel.

The empowering anointing can affect both our emotions and our physical strength. If our weaknesses are not under control, this anointing can stir up both. The empowering anointing can make us bold and aggressive but also vulnerable to spiritual attacks. The abiding anointing saves us from our magnified weaknesses which become exposed under the empowering anointing. Under the empowering anointing, dents in our armor can be exposed and highlighted, whether they are pride, sin, or something else. The abiding anointing keeps us safe after the empowering anointing lifts.

DISCUSSION QUESTIONS

1. What is the most important key to learning how to function in a prophetic anointing? Explain.

2. What are some ways the enemy can try and trick us into trading our anointing, like Esau did for something far less, trading the spiritual for the natural? What are some ways we can avoid the enemy's attempts to get us to trade in our anointings?

3. What are some good ways to know or figure out what our anointings are? Explain.

4. What are some ways we can increase or maximize the capacity of our anointings? Explain.

5. In your own words, define the abiding anointing. What is it for? What does it do?

6. Why is it so important that we value the abiding anointing above all others? Explain.

7. In your own words, define the empowering anointing. What is it for, and what does it do?

8. What are some of the ways we can know we have the abiding anointing? Explain.

9. What are some of the ways we can know we have an empowering anointing? Explain.

PROTECTING
the Prophetic

"For we do not wrestle against flesh and blood, but against principalities, against powers, against the rulers of the darkness of this age, against spiritual hosts of wickedness in the heavenly places" (Ephesians 6:12).

Ephesians 6:12 summarizes spiritual warfare. People are not our enemy; we are battling *spiritual* forces. Jesus Christ has given us authority over these forces. Spiritual warfare is about the forces of darkness in this realm trying to hinder the *koinonia* (fellowship) in the *ecclesia* (church). *Koinonia* is the unbreakable bond in the body of Christ.

Hell has a hierarchy, which is nothing more than a counterfeit angelic hierarchy. There are angels of the Lord that are "principalities." They are of a higher rank. "Powers" are also an angelic rank. When the angels fell from heaven, they continued their ranks. The saying, "higher levels, higher devils" is true. The bigger our assignment, the bigger the devils we must deal with. Angels are also assigned to us according to our assignment, ministry, and rank in the kingdom. The devil recognizes our spiritual rank and wants to unleash hell against us based on our rank.

FAMILIAR SPIRITS

There are several types of spirits we may encounter in spiritual warfare. Familiar spirits are spirits that work through personalities, families, and friends against God's purposes. They work through people and things that are familiar to us. They can even possess families. Addictions, alcohol, and perversion often riddle families and generational trees. Familiar spirits may be common, comfortable, or even familial to us.

Spirits that reside in generations are sometimes called "generational curses." I prefer to simply say that certain spirits find gateways into families. There are family members who open the door and invite or invoke certain types of spirits, like addictions, into families. Generationally speaking, family members who grow up around those atmospheres and environments can become familiar with the spirits that have attached themselves to their families.

Psychics and mediums often work through familiar spirits. If they gain information from familiar spirits, those spirits are from the dark side, who work through various personalities, friends, and family members, often without them realizing. The devil's biggest avenue for attacking us is through people and their words. By this, they try to stop God's will for our lives and will often use people who are most familiar to us.

A prime example of this is in Matthew 16 when Jesus began to announce that He would go to Jerusalem to be arrested and killed. Out of genuine concern, Simon Peter said, **"Far be it from You, Lord; this shall not happen to You!"** Jesus looked at Peter and said, **"Get behind Me, Satan!"** (see Matthew 16:22-23) Jesus was not calling Peter "Satan;" he was speaking to the spirit that spoke through Peter. The devil spoke through human concern to try and get Jesus to thwart God's will for Jesus to die for the sins

214

of the world. Jesus saw the spirit from hell behind the human face that was talking to Him. Satan will use well-intentioned people in our lives to try and thwart God's will for our lives. Sometimes those who are closest to us can hurt or hinder us the most. The enemy is constantly trying to exploit human relationships to pit us against one another.

The Lord can come and speak to us or communicate His thoughts to us through dreams about dear people in our lives. Be careful when you move into a new house because some houses are haunted. For example, a little girl may appear in a white flowing dress at the foot of your bed. The demonic can also appear through people we loved or people we were familiar with to make us comfortable, but as it continues, it gets much worse. Spirits will often first come to us in the personality of a familiar person, then later reveal their true colors.

THE LEVIATHAN SPIRIT

God will work and do things outside the walls of the church during this end-time reformation. However, preachers and worship leaders will not be the only ones anointed by God. The leviathan spirit (see Job 3:8, 40:15, 41:1-34; Psalm 74:14, 104:26; Isaiah 27:1) is a twisting, crooked, piercing serpent which cannot be drawn with a hook, nor can his tongue be wrangled with a cord. In other words, its tongue cannot be controlled.

Although this spirit is at work in the world right now, it has anointed certain political leaders and others to carry out its work. It is renowned for twisting people's words until our perceptions of them change. The leviathan spirit is at work in our media right now, where everything gets twisted. This is also the spirit of Marxism, socialism, and globalism that is being pushed on our nation and world right now. Its motives are currently being made clear in our education system and in other areas.

This is a spirit we are battling, not a person. The leviathan spirit is said to have six or seven heads, each of which may represent the following deadly sins the Lord hates:

> **These six things the Lord hates, yes, seven are an abomination to Him: A proud look, a lying tongue, hands that shed innocent blood, a heart that devises wicked plans, feet that are swift in running to evil, a false witness who speaks lies, and one who sows discord among brethren (Proverbs 6:16-19).**

Job 41:10 tells us that Leviathan is a spirit that can be stirred up. We must deal with this spirit with the sword of truth. The Spirit of truth is the only thing that can bring down the spirit of Leviathan with its twisting lies. My prayer to the Lord is that we, His people, will be armed with the full armor and weaponry of God. May He put His sword of truth in the hands of those who are assigned to deal with this spirit.

THE JEZEBEL SPIRIT

The Jezebel spirit cuts off the prophetic and causes it to hide. **"For so it was, while Jezebel massacred the prophets of the Lord, that Obadiah had taken one hundred prophets and hidden them, fifty to a cave, and had fed them with bread and water" (1 Kings 18:4).**

When you see prophetic ministries being attacked or maligned to their faces or behind their backs, or when people attack, demean, or diminish the prophetic ministry, just know this is the spirit of Jezebel that always tries to run the prophets into caves and shut them up. If the Jezebel spirit cannot kill the prophets, it will try to make them hide to shut them up.

Over the years, some in the church thought the Jezebel spirit influenced how people dressed, but it goes much deeper than that. 1 Kings 19:2 shows more about the Jezebel spirit: **"Then Jezebel sent a messenger to Elijah, saying, 'So let the gods do to me, and more also, if I do not make your life as the life of one of them by tomorrow about this time.'"** The Jezebel spirit also threatens, bullies, and manipulates the prophetic ministry. Threats and manipulation are two of the surest signs of both witchcraft and the Jezebel spirit.

Revelation 2:20 says, **"Nevertheless I have a few things against you, because you allow that woman Jezebel, who calls herself a prophetess, to teach and seduce My servants to commit sexual immorality and eat things sacrificed to idols."** The Jezebel spirit will try to get true prophetic ministries to mix with New Age paganism and the occult and then try to get the church to tolerate this. The prophetic is not about "getting in touch with our inner selves" or mediating through any other channel. Jesus is the *only* way. If we talk through any other source than Jesus, we are practicing witchcraft and will go to hell if we don't stop.

Sometimes I hear people preaching and using the same terminology found in New Age books that do not require Jesus. They are dabbling in witchcraft. Any ritual or process outside Jesus and the Holy Spirit must be removed from our midst. We don't need to get "in touch" with the spirit world. We should also take inventory of our libraries to make sure our books and authors don't follow other religions or other things outside of Jesus. Jezebel will pollute us. Don't let her seduce you with New Age mysticism. Do what they did in Acts 19:19 and burn those books!

A SPIRIT OF DIVINATION

"Now it happened, as we went to prayer, that a certain slave girl possessed with a spirit of divination met us, who brought her masters much profit by fortune-telling" (Acts 16:16). For several days, this girl conducted a vocal marketing campaign, giving free advertising to Paul and his ministry. However, Paul recognized the source. He did not want free advertising from hell. It may sound positive for the gospel or even the prophetic, but it's the antichrist spirit. It sounds like it favors Jesus, but it's really just trying to gain a larger audience.

When Paul used the name of Jesus on her, **"I command you in the name of Jesus Christ to come out of her"** (see Acts 16:18), the spirit of divination was driven out. The last thing we want in the prophetic are demonic endorsements and approval. We are all identified by our friends *and* our enemies. The demons told the truth about Paul, but he neither needed nor wanted their endorsement.

The spirit of divination is counterfeit to the prophetic, and it takes an apostolic or prophetic anointing to expose it. And if the Lord reveals it, He wants to heal it. A divination spirit will squeeze and choke when it's exposed. Recognize this when it happens. The spirit of divination is often confused with the true prophetic. Other times it's not the devil; it's just our flesh being carnal and needing to be circumcised (see Colossians 2:11).

CASTING OUT DEMONS

Jesus cast out demons by His own authority. Paul was careful to speak to demons only in the authority of Jesus Christ. Here, Paul spoke beyond the girl to the demon itself. **"And he came out that very hour"** (see Acts 16:18). Some spirits come out the minute we pray, others come out within the same hour, still others take longer. Some only come out by prayer and fasting (see Matthew 17:21). We don't know why; they just do. It could have to do with realms or ranks in the spirit. Acts 19:13-15 tells the story of the seven sons of Sceva.

> **Then some of the itinerant Jewish exorcists took it upon themselves to call the name of the Lord Jesus over those who had evil spirits, saying, "We exorcise you by the Jesus whom Paul preaches." Also there were seven sons of Sceva, a Jewish chief priest, who did so.**
>
> **And the evil spirit answered and said, "Jesus I know, and Paul I know; but who are you?"**
>
> **Then the man in whom the evil spirit was leaped on them, overpowered them, and prevailed against them, so that they fled out of that house naked and wounded.**

The seven sons of Sceva tried to use an authority they did not have. They tried to use Paul's authority without Paul's anointing. Don't try to usurp an authority you don't have and don't presume assignments God did not assign to you. You cannot operate in someone else's authority. If you do, you'll get a blowback from hell that will shock you. Just like we cannot preach someone else's sermon and get the same results.

We must have a connection with God as our source. That is the difference between the prophetic and the demonic. Paul spoke to demons only in the authority of Jesus Christ. Demons either know us, or they don't know us. Does hell perceive us as a threat? If so, we will experience warfare because we are a threat to the kingdom of darkness. If a demon hears your name, will he know you and your authority? The seven sons of Sceva ran out of the house naked. We need preachers, not streakers!

Sometimes what we call "spiritual warfare" is really just the consequences of our stupid decisions. That is called "carnality." We cannot rebuke the devil out of carnality. Instead, we must circumcise our flesh. We cannot operate in an authority we have not received from above. God must be our source.

I once ministered to a woman who started barking like a dog and whose eyes rolled up back into her head. As the pastor of the church, I just walked up to her. She said in a deep voice, "I know who you are." I said, "I bet you do know who I am, devil. And I bet you know someone better than I. In the name of Jesus Christ, come out!" She threw up seven times, and each time a demon came out, and she was delivered. We see this more often in other countries, but don't start looking for a demon under every bush.

A PRAYER FOR DELIVERANCE

Perhaps you need deliverance. If so, I want to pray for you to be free from anything that might be hindering you. Put your hand on your head or your heart and repeat this prayer:

"Father, in the name of Jesus, if there is any door I have opened in my life, knowingly or unknowingly, that has invited in the realm of darkness, an influence of darkness in my life in any way, I repent. I ask You to forgive me. I renounce, in the name of Jesus Christ, all spiritual practices outside the constraints of God's Word. I plead the blood of Jesus.

"Satan, you have no authority in my life, my family, or my home. I break any attachment or association with any form of the occult. In the name of Jesus Christ, I am free!"

Now praise the Lord.

A PRAYER FOR DELIVERANCE MINISTERS

I believe there are also people reading this right now who are prophetic ministers of deliverance. Gross darkness is in this world. Now, more than ever, we need people who have authority to expose and remove darkness from people's lives. We cannot talk, wish, or bribe demons out of people. We have spiritual authority to *remove* them. If you feel called to a true deliverance ministry, I also want to pray for you.

"I prophesy that God is raising up deliverance ministers in response to the level of darkness unleashed on earth in this hour. I pray that God will meet that need by raising up ministers of deliverance who will walk in a realm of authority that makes demons tremble when they are near. Your words, your demeanor, your atmosphere will make demons tremble. When demons speak, they will say, 'Jesus I know,' then like Paul, they will also speak your name because they also know you.

"So, right now, Lord, I believe You are raising up people as ministers of deliverance in this hour. I release an anointing for deliverance. Father, I pray this mantle of deliverance will come on boys, girls, men, and women who feel called and that they are given authority to address the works of darkness in regions, cities, and places of business. In the name of the Lord Jesus, I release that mantle of deliverance."

Now pray in the Spirit and receive that deliverance anointing. Prophetic and deliverance ministries were meant to go hand in hand. They have been severed far too long.

"The Lord says, 'I am responding to gross darkness on the earth by raising up a company of prophetic deliverance ministers to expose the authorities in the realm of darkness and in all spheres of influence. I will raise them up and the glory of the

Lord will shine upon them. They will shine like bright stars in the firmament, and I will show Myself to be strong and mighty through My prophetic deliverers, says the Holy Spirit.'

"The Lord says, 'Satan does not have the final say in your family, business, or personal economy. He does not have the final say in media, education, business, or the destiny of the United States of America. I am anointing people called to specific realms to walk in anointings of deliverance, to break the chains of darkness until the full day comes.'"

HOW JESUS OVERCAME TEMPTATION

Thomas Aquinas at the Council of Trent called the world, the flesh, and the devil "implacable enemies of the soul." We see all three of these being played out with Adam and Eve in the garden in Genesis 3, and also with Jesus' forty-day fast and temptations in the wilderness in Matthew 4.

> Then Jesus was led up by the Spirit into the wilderness to be tempted by the devil. And when He had fasted forty days and forty nights, afterward He was hungry. Now when the tempter came to Him, he said, "If You are the Son of God, command that these stones become bread."
>
> But He answered and said, "It is written, Man shall not live by bread alone, but by every word that proceeds from the mouth of God.'"
>
> Then the devil took Him up into the holy city, set Him on the pinnacle of the temple, and said to Him, "If You are the Son of God, throw Yourself down. For it is written:
>
> 'He shall give His angels charge over you,' and, 'In their hands they shall bear you up, Lest you dash your foot against a stone.'"

Jesus said to him, "It is written again, 'You shall not tempt the Lord your God.'"

Again, the devil took Him up on an exceedingly high mountain and showed Him all the kingdoms of the world and their glory.

And he said to Him, "All these things I will give You if You will fall down and worship me."

Then Jesus said to him, "Away with you, Satan! For it is written, 'You shall worship the Lord your God, and Him only you shall serve.'"

Then the devil left Him, and behold, angels came and ministered to Him (Matthew 4:1-11).

Jesus had just been baptized in the Jordan River by John. Up to this point He had done no recorded miracles. At His baptism, the heavens were opened, the voice of God the Father spoke, and the Holy Spirit descended and rested on Him like a dove. There's a difference between being filled with the Spirit and the Spirit "resting" on us. Jesus healed everyone He prayed for because the Spirit rested on Him. The Lord works through many but rests on few. This is also the difference between being filled with the Spirit and being mantled with the seven Spirits of God. The seven Spirits of God are the nine gifts of the Spirit in their full maturity.

Most unique to Jesus' baptism was the fact that the Father spoke audibly, **"This is My beloved Son, in whom I am well pleased."** God audibly spoke His identity over Him. "This *is* my beloved Son." The very thing the Father spoke over Him, affirming His identity, was the very thing Satan tested. "If you *are* the Son of God..." Satan will always test or question in the wilderness what God declared to us in the water. John the Baptist heard God say this and knew he could now decrease so Christ could increase (see John 3:30). Later, John asked his disciples to ask Jesus, **"Are you the Coming One, or do we look for another?"** (see Matthew 11:3) When in prison, he began to question what he once boldly knew.

God verbally identified Jesus as His Son, and Jesus identified Himself with us through His baptism and temptations. Jesus identified with broken humanity, while God identified Him with the Divine. Jesus was led by the Spirit into the wilderness. Jesus' temptations were necessary to show that He was much like, yet much unlike the first Adam. Jesus was tempted like Adam and Eve. The lust of the eyes and the lust of the flesh saw that the tree was good for food. The pride of life saw that the tree was desirable to make one wise (see Genesis 3:6; 1 John 2:16).

Jesus proved that no iniquity could be found in Him, though He was fully man. Iniquity was found in Lucifer, so Lucifer wanted to show that sin could also be found in man. However, Jesus proved him wrong by giving up His rights as God to do everything as a man in good standing with God. Jesus was the firstfruits of a new creation that could also have what He had (see 1 Corinthians 15:20, 23). Jesus needed to show that He was much like, yet much unlike the first Adam. Then, He showed us that we can also surrender our lives to God, following His example as the firstfruits of a new creation.

The contrast between the glory that followed Jesus' baptism and the challenge of His temptation with the enemy must be noted here. Whenever there is an increase or elevation in Holy Spirit activity, shortly thereafter, the devil will try to tempt us in our personal lives. To be overcomers, we must remain on guard whenever the supernatural increases in our lives. This is the cool waters of the Jordan versus the barren wilderness, the huge crowds versus the solitude of silence. The Holy Spirit rested on Him like a dove, then drove Him into the wilderness. This is the voice of the Father versus the hiss of the serpent, the waters of baptism versus the fires of the wilderness, the open heavens versus the portals of hell. The anointed was now the attacked.

Jesus did not need to be tempted to grow but rather to identify with us. He **"was in all points tempted, as we are, yet without sin"** (see Hebrews 4:15). He was born without a sin nature, so we could live without a sin nature when we are born again.

The Lord uses the ministry of Satan to prove us. Satan was put here to try the sons and daughters of God with temptations, trials, and warfare. Satan works for God but does not like to think of it that way (see Job 1:8). He can do nothing without God's permission. God restricted Satan's attack on Job (see Job 1:12). Satan can only go so far because God has him on a leash.

While we are generally tempted with lesser demons, Jesus' temptation was more severe. He dealt with Satan himself. Matthew 4:3 says, **"Now when the tempter came to Him..."** Not *if* but *when*. *Tempted* means to be tested or tried. Jesus entered the wilderness from a solid place. He was affirmed by the Father, He was pleasing to the Father, and He was identified by the Father during an open-heaven experience.

JESUS' FIRST TEMPTATION

Satan said, **"If you are the son of God...."** Satan will try to make us question what God has declared or what God has given us through visions and dreams. Our circumstances do not always seem to match the promises of God. Faith sustains us until they become reality.

Don't be shocked by Satan's two-letter word, "if." He wants us to put a question mark where God put a period. He did the same to Adam and Eve. We must see the difference between Adam's response and Jesus' response. Instead of falling for Satan's questions, respond like Jesus did. Stop the questions and tell the devil what God's Word says. Our faith and our responses to temptation should not be grounded in circumstances but grounded in God's Word.

When Jesus fasted, His first temptation was, **"Command that these stones become bread"** (see Matthew 4:3). This is tied to what we can and cannot do or to what the spirit of religion *wants* us to do. Our works become the enemy's target rather than our identity in Christ. This first temptation was to use God's gifts for selfish reasons, to provide food for Himself.

If we give in to this, we will live on a spiritual rollercoaster. Satan tried to get Him to use His gifts for selfish purposes, not to turn stones to riches, rubies, or gold but simply to bread. No matter what your current state is, whether you have sinned or not, don't let Satan make you question your identity in Christ.

We must let God exalt us, not ourselves. When God uses you, downplay it. When we feel the need to brag about what God is doing through us, because we need Him to affirm us or make up for a deficiency in our ego, that is the first temptation every anointed prophetic person must overcome.

Don't be tempted to use your giftings to benefit you; that is *not* prophetic. In fact, it becomes witchcraft when we use our giftings to manipulate circumstances to our advantage. You will be tested in this way. Ask yourself, "Why am I bragging about these things?" Satan wasn't trying to get Jesus to turn stones into rubies or gold, but when Satan asked a question, Jesus said, "No." When we start comparing ourselves to others, that's a sure sign we are using our gifts to gain acceptance. We may have been rejected in the past, or we may just want others to see how God has blessed us, but that is just immaturity.

Jesus proved His strength and anointing would not become His trap. Some people in prophetic ministry let their identities become tied to their anointings, their preaching, their singing, or their traveling. However, this leads to nothing healthy. It wasn't that Jesus refused supernatural help to feed Himself. He was more than happy to eat when the angels brought Him food at the end of His forty-day fast. It was more about obeying and submitting to the Father.

Jesus' reply to each temptation was, "It is written…" He relied on the Word of God written in His heart to overcome. He could have banished Satan to another galaxy if he wanted, but He instead chose to resist him in a way that we could relate to as humans. Read the Word. Something is deposited in us every time we do. This is one of the most important spiritual disciplines we can have. Read it and consume it. Jesus said, **"The words that I speak to you are spirit, and they are life"** (see John 6:63). We cannot banish Satan to Mars, but we can say "No" to him.

Our real motive for fasting the way the Lord asked us to is to get us to hunger more for the words that proceed from the mouth of God than we do for physical food—to hunger more for spiritual food, which is not easy. Jesus relied on God's Word to feed and sustain Him in ways that natural food could not.

JESUS' SECOND TEMPTATION

"If you are the Son of God, throw Yourself down. For it is written, 'He shall give His angels charge over you.'" Here, Satan quoted Psalm 91. Jesus was anointed *before* the temptation but was proven *through* the temptation. He was not only anointed, but He was now also worthy of authority.

Many anointed people have no authority. The anointing is a gift, but the authority we are entrusted with comes by overcoming. Satan appealed to Jesus' human desire to gain public approval. Every anointed prophetic person will be tempted in this way. "Show them what you can do," Satan will suggest. We are gratified by public approval, especially when that approval is demonstrated to and seen by those who have judged us.

The pinnacle of the temple rose some two hundred feet from the floor of the Kidron Valley. A leap from there would have made a remarkable spectacle, but it also would have been a self-induced crisis. The devil loves "drama queens" who want people to recognize them. They love to be the center of attention and to show others what they know or can do. These are the methods false messiahs use to gain the "oohs and ahs" of the public. This was Simon the Sorcerer's motive (see Acts 8:18-20).

But Jesus said, "It is written..." Satan in turn pulled a Scripture from Psalm 91, but left out some important words, **"For He shall give His angels charge over you, <u>to keep you in all your ways</u>" (see Psalm 91:11).** He misquoted it by leaving out a key phrase. A text taken out of "con-text" is just a "con." Satan tried to make a promise out of what was never a promise.

Satan also took what God said to Adam out of context. God said, **"Of every tree of the garden you may freely eat; but of the tree of the knowledge of good and evil, you shall not eat, for in the day that you eat of it you shall surely die" (see Genesis 2:16-17).** Eve misquoted this by adding, **"God has said, 'You shall not eat of it, <u>nor shall you touch it</u>, lest you die'" (see Genesis 3:3).** We must never add to or take away from God's Word (see Deuteronomy 12:32; Revelation 22:18-19).

But then Satan deceived her saying, **"Has God indeed said...? You will not surely die. For God knows when eat of it your eyes will be opened, and you will be like God, knowing**

good and evil" (see Genesis 3:1, 4-5). The spirit of religion twists the word of God by over and under emphasizing certain parts to make it of no effect (see Matthew 15:6). Here, God's word was not used to teach or encourage but to deceive. Satan misapplied God's word, and Eve failed the test.

Since Jesus was secure in His identity, He did not misuse the promise of the text to get God to prove His love and concern for Him by jumping off the temple pinnacle. We should not use the Bible or God's promises to prove that God should do what we ask Him to do. We ask humbly. Jesus can heal today because the cross provided us the means to destroy the works of the devil, including sickness and disease. This is not about making God prove His love for us by "cashing in" on God's promises for every and any situation.

JESUS' THIRD TEMPTATION

"All these things I will give You if You will fall down and worship me." Here, Satan went further in his temptations. This was a satanic temptation to rule the world by taking a shortcut around the cross. How conceited and arrogant of Satan to say, "If you'll fall down and worship me, I'll give the earth, which You created, back to You." Satan tempted Him with this because, even before his fall, Satan loved worship (see Isaiah 14:11-14). Satan knew Jesus was promised rulership of the world, but desired worship so much he was willing to give up those kingdoms, just to see Jesus worship him. That is how conceited our enemy is; he never understood why he was kicked out of heaven in the first place. Jesus resisted him again, and Satan left.

"Therefore submit to God. Resist the devil and he will flee from you" (James 4:7). We must first submit ourselves to God, or we will be operating in our own strength. However, after we overcome, angelic power will be released!

At the end of Jesus' forty-day fast, the angels came and ministered to Him. If you are going through trials right now, stand on God's Word, don't let the circumstances get to you, and angelic realms will be released to you. Pass the test of fiery trials— children, church issues, whatever—and you will receive authority when you overcome. The Lord will release angelic activity into your life.

This is my prayer for you: "Lord, help each of us to be equipped with visions, dreams, and more spiritual authority. I release over us to come up one step higher in our prophetic giftings. Lord, release an anointing for deliverers to become overcomers. We want Your authority to work in the anointings in our lives. Overcomers will sit with You in Your Father's throne."

DISCUSSION QUESTIONS

1. In what ways does Ephesians 6:12 summarize spiritual warfare? Explain.

2. In your own words, how would you describe familiar spirits? What is their main role and purpose? Explain.

3. How would you describe the leviathan spirit? What is its main function and purpose? Can you name any contemporary examples of the leviathan spirit? Why do you think this spirit is so prevalent today?

4. How would you define the Jezebel spirit? What is its main role and function? How can prophetic people especially protect themselves from a Jezebel spirit?

5. What is most important to know before attempting to cast out demons? Explain.

6. Do you feel called to deliverance ministry? Why or why not?

7. What stood out to you the most about how Jesus overcame temptation in the wilderness? Explain.

8. How was Jesus' handling of temptation in the wilderness different from that of Adam and Eve in the garden? Explain.

9. What similarities and differences do you see in the three temptations Jesus experienced in the wilderness?

10. What do you think is the biggest key to overcoming all temptation? Explain.

11. Why is overcoming temptation so important to prophetic ministry?

"The heart of true last-days ministry will be ministry to the Lord in the secret place."

PARTNERING WITH
the Prophetic

Not all prophetic people are in the office of the prophet. However, Paul said that we should all **"desire spiritual gifts, but especially that we may prophesy,"** and that **"we can all prophesy" (see I Corinthians 14:1, 31).** The gift of prophecy is for all. It is available to all God's people, though most are not walking in it.

> And I fell at his feet to worship him. But he said to me, "See that you do not do that! I am your fellow servant, and of your brethren who have the testimony of Jesus. Worship God! For the testimony of Jesus is the spirit of prophecy (Revelation 19:10-11).

THE PROPHETIC TESTIMONY

John was in a glory realm when he had this encounter with a "fellow servant." John fell at the feet of his fellow servant in the Lord. I believe we also will have encounters where we experience holy terror and a holy awe of the Lord. Since fatherlessness has increased in the world, some people describe their godly encounters as "just crawling up on Papa's lap." That's fine. God is a loving Father. However, there is also the severity of God. We must stand in both the goodness *and* the severity of God and not get in the ditch on one side of the road or the other. Severity can become legalism, and grace can become hyper-grace.

When we behold the God of heaven, we will fall on our faces. When Isaiah was in God's presence, he said, **"Woe is me, for I am undone! Because I am a man of unclean lips, and I dwell in the midst of a people of unclean lips. For my eyes have seen the King, the Lord of hosts" (see Isaiah 6:5).** There's just something about the presence of God that reveals our fallen human nature, yet simultaneously makes us more like Him. We identify with the new man in Christ.

Whenever we move in the gifts, anointings, or spirit of prophecy, it produces a testimony, meaning the Spirit bears witness with our spirit that Jesus is Lord (see Romans 8:16). Psychics are not godly. They neither lift up nor glorify the Lord. They are false witnesses, because they do not testify of Jesus. True prophecy will do one of three things—bring people into their divine purpose, bring people into a greater experience with God, or bring people into divine healing.

We see this in Acts 9 when Saul had his Damascus Road experience. Saul was persecuting the church and had letters in hand to imprison Christians in Damascus. On his way to Damascus, a light shined from heaven and blinded him on the road. Then, in Damascus, the Lord spoke to a prophetic voice there named Ananias. By revelation, Ananias was instructed to go lay hands on Saul because he was a chosen vessel. Ananias initially did not want to, because he had heard terrible things about Saul. The Lord told Ananias to go to a street named Straight and to a specific house of a person named Judas. Then, when Ananias prayed for Paul, he was healed and filled with the Holy Spirit.

So, by New Testament prophetic revelation, someone totally unrelated to Saul was given a person's name, the street he was on, the specific house he would be in, and a divine purpose. When

Ananias arrived, a testimony was produced by the spirit of prophecy that functioned through Ananias, and Saul was healed.

The testimony of the spirit of prophecy was seen three ways: 1) Saul received divine healing through the prophetic, 2) Saul was filled with the Spirit and received a greater encounter with the Lord through the prophetic, and 3) Ananias prophesied to Saul that he would become an apostle to the gentiles, so Saul found his purpose through the prophetic. The testimony was that a man with letters from religious leaders who persecuted Christians ended up writing letters to Christians and teaching them how to live Christian lives. The purpose of developing a prophetic anointing gift is ultimately to glorify the name of Jesus.

If the prophetic testimony is not tied to the true Spirit of Jesus, it's just spiritualism. Psychics don't testify of Jesus. The Greek word translated *testimony* is *marturia*, which means "evidence, record, report," or "proof in a judicial sense." As developing prophets, our words must testify to and lift up Jesus. Prophetic words must always provide evidence of the testimony of Jesus for healing, purpose, or greater encounters. In fact, the sole purpose of the Holy Spirit is to reveal, lift up, and magnify Jesus. The testimony will provide the evidence. Don't just tell us you're prophetic; show us by your fruit.

THE MAKING OF A PROPHET

The prophetic testimony will also bring persecution to those who carry this witness. Revelation 1:9 says, **"I, John, both <u>your brother and companion in the tribulation</u> and kingdom and patience of Jesus Christ, was on the island that is called Patmos for the word of God and <u>for the testimony of Jesus Christ</u>."** The level of persecution that can be unleashed on those in prophetic ministry is staggering.

Sadly, it most often comes from those closest to us. They'll say things like, "You're getting off into the occult." "This is New Age." "This is fake." "It's staged." "It's too extreme." The prophetic anointing *will* attract persecution. Attacks and criticisms will come. Get ready for it! Many Christians do not believe in supernatural gifts. Others will judge what we're doing because it's different from what they're used to. We must not take this personally.

"Blessed are you when they revile and persecute you, and say all kinds of evil against you falsely for My sake. Rejoice and be exceedingly glad, for great is your reward in heaven, for so they persecuted the prophets who were before you" (Matthew 5:11-12).

"Remember the word that I said to you, 'A servant is not greater than his master.' If they persecuted Me, they will also persecute you" (see John 15:20). It *will* happen to you. You will be maligned by other church members and family members because you're going after the deeper things of God. The apostle John said he was our "brother and companion" in tribulation. He was exiled to an island where he could not prophesy to anyone. So, he sat alone with the Lord and wrote letters to the churches.

The prophetic temperament requires us to be assertive and take a stand even when pressure comes. Many want to be prophetic until the rejection comes. However, the greater the rejection, the greater the anointing, because God uses rejects. I am a prime example of this. Joseph was cast into a pit by his brothers because he had prophetic dreams. David was also rejected by his own brothers.

The people who have most altered history had to go through dark times. We may have to go through dark times of rejection. It's like the crushing of the olives where the oil comes out after they're squeezed. Jesus, the stone which the builders rejected, has been made by the Father the chief cornerstone of the church (see Psalm 118:22; Acts 4:11). God exalted Him after men rejected Him. We must go through the same rejection. The rejection is what made Jesus the chief cornerstone. Sometimes, we must be rejected by men to be exalted by God.

STAND FIRM ON THE PROPHETIC

We will overcome if we hold on to the prophetic testimony. Revelation 12:11 says, **"And they overcame him by the blood of the Lamb and by the word of their testimony, and they did not love their lives to the death."** The prophetic anointing testifies of Jesus to our world and to the people for whom we pray and prophesy.

To walk in this anointing and stand firm on the testimony of Jesus, we cannot love our lives or overly care about others' opinions. Rather, we must hold on to the prophetic testimony because it has overcoming power. When we give a prophetic word to someone from the spirit of prophecy and they are healed, walk in their purpose, or receive revelation, a testimony is produced. Those testimonies are what we must hold on to when all hell, persecution, and criticism come against us. Hold on to the testimony! Maybe you had a dream or a word of knowledge. Hold on to the fruit of those prophetic words, because this must be valued more than what other people or other churches think of us.

We must value the prophetic testimony above the validating testimonies of leaders, churches, or denominations. The prophetic testimony must matter to us more than any negative testimony coming from other churches or ministries that speak against us. You will face rejection because you have "Urim" and "Thummim" (see Exodus 28:20; Leviticus 8:8; Ezra 2:63). This means you have revelation and truth in your priestly breastplate, which is the discernment of the Holy Spirit. Your peace should be valued more than anything else. The enemy will try to steal your peace. Jesus prayed in the garden of Gethsemane to overcome this battle with His flesh. When He prayed, he sweat drops of blood (see Luke 22:44), yet he prayed, **"Not My will, but Yours, be done"** (see Luke 22:42). He began flowing in the Spirit, and the sweat in His flesh ended.

The dragon will seek you out to make war with you because of the prophetic voice and testimony that exists in you and because of your ability to reproduce seed. The enemy wants to destroy our ability to train and equip others. We are raising up a mighty end-time army. Revelation 12:17 says, **"And the dragon was enraged with the woman, and he went to make war with the rest of her offspring, who keep the commandments of God and have the testimony of Jesus Christ."** The testimony of Jesus is the spirit of prophecy. That is what attracts the dragon to seek us out and make war with us, because we have the testimony of Jesus and are reproducing offspring.

When God gives us a prophecy for others, that word is not only for us and them but also for our children and their children. Sometimes we're seeing an apple seed when God is seeing an apple orchard. Claim every prophecy you receive for your household also. The prophetic is generational. Elisha became who Elijah was. Whom we align ourselves with matters. In the Gospels and in Acts, the nobleman, Cornelius, and the Philippian jailer's entire households were saved. **"You and all your household will be saved"** (see John 4:53; Acts 11:14, 16:31).

STRENGTH IN PROPHETIC COMPANIES

We are also strengthened in a prophetic company. When the dragon is attacking us or we are rejected, we can overcome better together in a prophetic company. 1 Samuel 19:20 says, **"Then Saul sent messengers to take David. And when they saw the group of prophets prophesying, and Samuel standing as leader over them, the Spirit of God came upon the messengers of Saul, and they also prophesied."** Samuel was appointed as leader over them, meaning they were guided and did all things together. Even their enemies started prophesying when the prophetic school or company was together. When the enemy comes against one, he comes against all. When the enemy comes against you as a company, the Holy Spirit hits back.

It's important to be part of a prophetic order, so we can stand together. There's just something about being in a prophetic company. Few prophets in history have been able to stand by themselves. Could it be that when prophetic companies stand together, like Saul's messengers, or like on the day of Pentecost, the world gets so zapped by the Holy Spirit that they want what we have, and God pours out His Spirit on *all* flesh? To win Saul's messengers requires more than theological debate; it requires a move of the Holy Spirit. When companies of prophets stand together, greater outpourings ensue.

The schools of the prophets in Scripture dealt with poetry, history, and the social and political issues of their day. The prophets spoke guidance, even knowing what the enemy was planning in his own bedroom (see 2 Kings 6:12). God wants to raise up prophetic companies. When kings were coronated, the prophets were there. Samuel anointed Saul to be king. Samuel anointed David to be king. The prophets were frequently found at the house of God together. They had a gathering place. 2 Kings 2:3 says, **"Now the sons of the prophets who were at Bethel came out to Elisha, and said to him, 'Do you know that the Lord will take away your master from over you today?'"** They were at Bethel, the "house of God," together.

The prophetic testimony and prophetic companies are even strengthened when they eat together. 2 Kings 4:38 says, **"And Elisha returned to Gilgal, and there was a famine in the land. Now the sons of the prophets were sitting before him; and he said to his servant, 'Put on the large pot, and boil stew for the sons of the prophets.'"** Let's eat together!

The prophetic testimony and prophetic companies are even stronger when they move and build together. 2 Kings 6:1 says, **"And the sons of the prophets said to Elisha, 'See now, the place where we dwell with you is too small for us. Please, let us go the Jordan, and let every man take a beam from there, and let us make there a place where we may dwell.'"** God is raising up a prophetic order, a new breed, that will build together, prophesy together, and see miracles happen together. This was when the axe head fell off the axe into the water and Elisha brought it back to the surface. They saw miracles together. Strange, crazy, and even bizarre miracles happen when prophetic companies work together.

This prophetic anointing and testimony is transferable from senior prophetic voices. Numbers 11:25 demonstrates this with Moses and the elders,

> **"Then the Lord came down in the cloud, and spoke to him, and took of the Spirit that was upon him, and placed the same upon the seventy elders; and it happened, when the Spirit rested upon them, that they prophesied, although they never did so again."**

The Lord Himself came down and put this prophetic anointing and testimony on the entire company.

There is an anointing in mature prophetic leadership. Deuteronomy 34:9 says, **"Now Joshua the son of Nun was full of the spirit of wisdom, for Moses had laid his hands on him;**

so the children of Israel heeded him, and did as the Lord had commanded Moses." Moses laid hands on Joshua, and Joshua increased in his anointing and authority with the people through the laying on of Moses' hands.

1 Samuel 10:6 says, "Then the Spirit of the Lord will come upon you, and you will prophesy with them and be turned into another man." When the prophetic anointing and testimony come on you, you may be hit with such prophetic power that people see you as a different person.

The prophetic anointing and testimony are also birthed when ministers of music sing or play instruments. There is a connection between worship, music, and the prophetic. In 2 Kings 3:15, Elisha said, "'But now bring me a musician.' Then it happened, when the musician played, that the hand of the Lord came upon him." There's just something about atmospheres of worship that bring prophetic anointings and produce testimonies in people's lives.

DISCUSSION QUESTIONS

1. In your own words, what is meant by "the testimony of Jesus is the spirit of prophecy" (see Revelation 19:11)?

2. Name some of the things that separate psychics, spiritualists, and New Age practitioners from true prophets.

3. Describe the three purposes for the prophetic as seen in Saul's road to Damascus experience (see Acts 9:10-12, 15-18).

4. Why do you think the prophetic arouses such high levels of tribulation and persecution? Explain.

5. Why does a prophetic temperament require us to be assertive and take a stand? Explain.

6. When we give someone a personal prophecy, the prophecy goes beyond us and them. Who does this mean and why is that?

7. According to 1 Samuel 19:20 and Acts 2, what are some of the things that can happen when prophets come together in unity and form a company of prophets?

8. What are some of the things a company of prophets can do that individual prophets *cannot* do?

PASTORING
the Prophetic

John answered and said, "A man can receive nothing unless it has been given to him from heaven. You yourselves bear me witness, that I said, 'I am not the Christ,' but, 'I have been sent before Him.' He who has the bride is the bridegroom; but the friend of the bridegroom, who stands and hears him, rejoices greatly because of the bridegroom's voice. Therefore this joy of mine is fulfilled. He must increase, but I must decrease" (John 3:27-30).

Here, John the Baptist was describing what Jesus must have been feeling emotionally at the time when he said, **"He who has the bride is the bridegroom."** To understand what John said, they had to understand who Jesus was. The bride was God's people; the groom was Jesus. **"Let us be glad and rejoice and give Him glory, for the marriage of the Lamb has come, and His wife has made herself ready"** (Revelation 19:7)

"He who has the bride..." Jesus has a bride in His heart because God promised Him a prepared bride at the end of history. This bride is without spot or wrinkle, because she is not sitting but is active in prayer, intercession, and godly works. She does not do anything that might stain her garments. We can become clean and free from spots by asking the Lord to forgive and cleanse us. If you feel like the heat has been turned up on you lately, that might be God trying to iron out the wrinkles. God is seeking a bride who is ready.

We the church are a John the Baptist forerunner company, coming in the spirit and power of Elijah. We are a company of people with different names in the natural, who are coming in the spirit of Elijah. This is about more than just the prophetic and more than just turning the hearts of the fathers to the children and the hearts of the children to their fathers (see Malachi 4:5-6). This is about the spirit and power of Elijah turning the hearts of all ages back to one another and speaking life to one another. There is something powerful about a cross-generational movement.

The spirit of Elijah turns hearts, but it is Jesus the bridegroom who, with tender love, burns with a jealous desire for His people. Jesus is the One who has the bride, and we are His bridal company. He is looking for those who will hear His voice and be faithful to their calling. Jesus is chasing and running after a company that is without spot or wrinkle.

CARING FOR THE BRIDE

John described his ministry and lifestyle as "the friend of the bridegroom, who stands and hears Him." What does the life of a forerunner look like? Like the best man at a wedding. He does not seek the bride's attention. He is there to stand with the bridegroom during the most important decision of his life. He is there to prepare her to receive the love of the bridegroom.

> **For we do not preach ourselves, but Christ Jesus the Lord, and ourselves your <u>bondservants for Jesus' sake</u>. For it is the God who commanded light to shine out of darkness, who has shone in our hearts to give the light of the knowledge of**

the glory of God in the face of Jesus Christ (2 Corinthians 4:5).

But I trust in the Lord Jesus to send Timothy to you shortly, that I also may be encouraged when I know your state. For I have no one like-minded, <u>who will sincerely care for your state</u>. For all seek their own, not the things which are of Christ Jesus." (Philippians 2:19)

Paul cared deeply about the state of the people and wanted others who were pure, like Timothy, to help him. Too many seek their own. Those who help secure the bride for the bridegroom are not interested in drawing attention to themselves. The Lord, in a broader sense, is bringing down celebrity Christianity in our day.

The greatest gift we can give to the bridegroom is to refuse to participate in spiritual showmanship. The difference makers are those who are not interested in drawing people to themselves but rather pointing them to Jesus. The greatest gift the best man can give to the groom is not to draw the bride to himself. We don't need showman Christians! Instead, we prepare people to receive Jesus' embrace as their bridegroom God by empowering them to walk out the first commandment. In other words, we make sure the wedding happens. God is looking for this in a friend of the bridegroom company.

I sleep, but my heart is awake; it is the voice of my beloved! He knocks, saying, "Open for me, my sister, my love, my dove, my perfect one; for my head is covered with dew, my locks with the drops of the night."

I have taken off my robe; how can I put it on again? I have washed my feet; how can I defile them? My beloved put his hand by the latch of the door, and my heart yearned for him. I arose to open for my beloved, and my hands dripped

with myrrh, my fingers with liquid myrrh, on the handles of the lock.

I opened for my beloved, but my beloved had turned away and was gone. My heart leaped up when he spoke. I sought him, but I could not find him; I called him, but he gave me no answer. The watchmen who went about the city found me. They struck me, they wounded me; the keepers of the walls took my veil away from me. I charge you, O daughters of Jerusalem, if you find my beloved, that you tell him I am lovesick! (Song of Solomon 5:2-8)

God is putting His love as a seal on our hearts. This is what the Lord seeks—that we will not hurt or wound the bride. The true last-days ministry will not be on a stage in front of thousands. It will be ministry to the Lord in the secret place, preparing ourselves with myrrh. Some of the greatest prophetic words will be personal words. Some words will even be spoken in secret places to keep them pure before the Lord. We are to minister to the Lord.

When we minister to the Lord, ministry to people comes naturally. Ministry is vertical, then horizontal, the first and then the second commandment. John 3 says the friend of the bridegroom **"stands"** and hears him. This means diligent attentiveness to stand in God's presence in prayer and in the Word. Jeremiah 23:18 says, **"For who has stood in the counsel of the Lord, and has perceived and heard His word? Who has marked His word and heard it?"** The Word of God must mark us.

FRIENDS OF THE BRIDEGROOM

"Hears him" means we grow in the revelation of Jesus as the bridegroom. When was the last time we heard the Lord's voice, and it had a powerful impact on us? The clearest example of the prophetic is those who hear the bridegroom's voice, interpret it correctly, and apply it at the appropriate time.

John said the friend of the bridegroom also **"rejoices greatly because of the bridegroom's voice.... therefore this joy of mine is fulfilled."** John's joy was not in his own name or in his fivefold ministry capacity but in hearing His voice! When we hear His voice, nothing else can take its place. If we do not have joy unspeakable when we hear His voice, He has not become our magnificent obsession.

This is my prayer for you: "May you receive a release of the joy of the Lord in your life, so you can rejoice and have joy in your life again! I pray that the joy of the Lord will empower you through a revelation of the bridegroom, even if you're something like a John the Baptist figure, who lives in a desert or lives a simple lifestyle. I pray His voice will restore in you the joy of the Lord."

Isaiah prophesied of forerunners who would prepare the way for the Lord in the end times or at the time of Jesus' second coming when all flesh shall see Jesus' glory together.

The voice of one crying in the wilderness: "Prepare the way of the Lord; make straight in the desert a highway for our God. Every valley shall be exalted and every mountain and hill brought low; the crooked places shall be made straight and the rough places smooth; the glory of the Lord shall be revealed, and all flesh shall see it together; for the mouth of the Lord has spoken." (Isaiah 40:3-5)

"He said: 'I am the voice of one crying in the wilderness: make straight the way of the Lord,' as the prophet Isaiah said" (John 1:23).

John the Baptist was a down payment or partial fulfillment of Isaiah's prophecy. Forerunners prepare the way of the Lord by preparing people to know the way of the Lord and to respond rightly to Jesus in the end times. God raises up forerunners as mercy ministers to the multitudes just before the intensity of the Lord's end-time activities begin in both positive (revival) and negative (judgmental) ways.

This highway that God travels on is the voluntary agreement of His people as they partner with Him. Forerunners make sense of what is about to happen before the Spirit releases it globally. They are messengers who proclaim now what the Spirit will soon emphasize universally. They are one short step ahead of what the Spirit will soon release openly. This is why they are called "forerunners."

THE END-TIME FORERUNNERS MINISTRY

Jeremiah 12:5 speaks of forerunners, **"If you have run with the footmen, and they have wearied you, then how can you contend with horses? And if in the land of peace, in which you trusted, they wearied you, then how will you do in the floodplain of the Jordan?"**

If times are still good and you're already getting tired and barely hanging on, how will you handle bad times? If a foot race tires you, what will you do when things speed up and it becomes a horse race? We can't always be playing catch up! We need forerunners who are ahead of the race. A forerunner ministry doesn't make sense to the multitudes until intense activities begin. The wisdom of Noah's ark was not apparent until it began to rain. God wants to give you a second wind! I speak the Spirit of life over you!

Forerunners are messengers with voices who deliver specific messages to various spheres of influence. They are preachers, evangelists, artists, singers, musicians, actors, writers, media influencers, marketplace intercessors, or just people who make disciples one-on-one in churches, marketplaces, school campuses, and homes. Moms are among the most important forerunners.

> **Oh, that you would bear with me in a little folly—and indeed you do bear with me. For I am jealous for you with godly jealousy. For I have betrothed you to one husband, that I may present you as a chaste virgin to Christ. But I fear, lest somehow, as the serpent deceived Eve by his craftiness, so your minds may be corrupted from the simplicity that is in Christ. For if he who comes preaches another Jesus whom we have not preached, or if you receive a different spirit which you have not received, or a different gospel which you have not accepted—you may well put up with it! (2 Corinthians 11:1-4)**

Paul was jealous for God's people with a godly jealousy. He had betrothed them! The ministry of the friend of the bridegroom is to present us as a chaste virgin. Song of Solomon 8:6 says, **"Set me as a seal upon your heart, as a seal upon your arm; for love is as strong as death, jealousy as cruel as the grave; its flames are flames of fire, a most vehement flame."**

Paul said he was jealous with a godly jealousy for the affections of the Corinthians' hearts. He was like a friend of the bridegroom who watched out for the bride between the betrothal (engagement) and the wedding. He did his best to present the church, Jesus' bride, as a chaste virgin to Christ.

The friend of the bridegroom was to procure a virgin for the bridegroom, then guard her and bear testimony to her corporeal and marital endowment. It was upon this testimony the bridegroom chose his bride. The friend was the *internuncio,* or messenger, between her and her spouse-elect, carrying all messages between them, because before marriage, women were strictly guarded at home by their parents and friends.

The friend told him about her and her about him and passed along all messages. In Jewish culture, the bridegroom trusted his friend to do all these things. *Adam Clarke's Commentary on the Bible* says the friend was "to vindicate the purity of the bride." The virgin must remain a virgin during the betrothal, or it was considered adultery even before marriage. An engagement was considered a marriage that had not yet been consummated. Any time we give our hearts to someone or something other than God, it is like committing spiritual adultery during our betrothal.

> **"Behold, I will send you Elijah the prophet before the coming of the great and dreadful day of the Lord. And he will turn the hearts of the fathers to the children, and the hearts of the children to their fathers, lest I come and strike the earth with a curse" (Malachi 4:5-6).**

John the Baptist was the down payment of this prophecy. Today's end-time forerunners are its fulfillment. The seriousness of this betrothal seems way out of touch with today's culture, but the Lord is jealous for His bride. We need to pray, "Lord, we repent of anything that takes our eyes off You or builds us up instead. We want to stand and hear Your voice. We are here to preserve the bride's purity. We want to be a people living a pure life for You, as Your possession. You are the bridegroom, God, and we will not be seduced by or drawn to another gospel. We will remain faithful to You."

THREE LEVELS OF INTERPRETING SCRIPTURE

God gives us pictures. We call these pictures "types and shadows." The Old Testament is full of them. The Old Testament law prophesied New Testament realities. One reason God gave us New Testament truths in Old Testament stories was so that, as we read and study them, we'll understand that these stories were not only fulfilled but were also recorded thousands of years earlier. These pictures become so clear, especially when the Holy Spirit illuminates them for us. In this story of the bride and bridegroom, God acted deliberately and specifically, though He veiled the fullness of His purpose until His Son, who was to be the bridegroom, came.

Jesus condemned the Pharisees for being able to discern the weather by the color of the sky but not being able to discern how all the Scriptures they knew and memorized pointed to Him. They had veils over their eyes. They could not see the fullness of the story, which came when His Son came for His bride.

We now see the biblical structure provides the seeds of truth in the Old Testament, and the New Testament provides the harvest of those seeds, including the full revelation we will receive in this age. The seeds of truth are in the Old Testament through all kinds of stories, but these stories were only types and shadows or dramas acting out New Testament truths, which point to the greater realities.

For example, people have observed the Sabbath and feast days. We can honor and celebrate those days without being bound to their legalities. What does the Sabbath mean? It meant that they rested one day a week; that was the seed. The Jews are stuck holding on to the seed's meaning. However, the Sabbath was only a picture of the rest we are given in Christ Jesus from the labor of works of the flesh (see Isaiah 28:12; Hebrews 4:1-16). We are to lay down the works of the flesh and enter a posture of rest, seated with Him in heavenly places.

The Old Testament stories are often dramas acting out New Testament realities. Another popular saying is, "the Old

Testament is the New Testament concealed; the New Testament is the Old Testament revealed." The Old Testament stories all point to Christ, who *is* the greater reality. They could not see the full picture in the Old Testament. Sometimes we find ourselves in parts of a story, then leave it to God to help us find the rest. For example, in the story of David and Goliath, we might think, "I'm David, and my problems are Goliath," but there's always a greater reality in these stories that points to Christ and His first and second coming. Christ is the total fulfillment of all the Scriptures.

When we apply these stories to our lives, the fullness may or may not come. Parts of the stories may apply to us, while other parts may not. However, we should not throw out the baby with the bath water. Instead, we should find ourselves in these stories, apply their truths to our lives, but leave it to God whether and how much these stories come to pass, knowing that Christ is the sum total and fulfillment of all.

How can we interpret the meanings of these stories? How can we identify the people and symbols in these stories to discern their prophetic meanings? Some preachers are storytellers. Others can passionately apply a few Scriptures to our lives, while still others can fully interpret how they apply to our lives *and* how they point to Christ. For example, the woman with the issue of blood could have three layers of interpretation (see Matthew 9:20-22):

1. Simply reading or retelling the story.

2. This woman went to doctors for twelve years. No one could help her. She pressed through the crowd. Jesus healed her. Jesus can do the same for you.

3. Who does this woman represent? Who do the doctors represent? What does her bleeding represent? What does the

crowd represent? What does touching the hem of His garment represent?

The woman represents an unproductive church that is bleeding in its most intimate parts. She goes from meeting to meeting, then finally comes to Jesus for healing. She presses through to Jesus who heals her most intimate parts. Twelve years represents centuries of broken foundations from the church not being able to help people.

THE STORY OF ISAAC AND REBEKAH

Now, let's look at the story of Isaac and Rebekah using this third layer of interpretation. It is helpful to read the entire story to get the full picture. Abraham is a picture of God the Father. Then there's a servant. We assume this servant is Eliezer, since Eliezer was Abraham's servant for many years. However, the servant is not mentioned by name in this story. He is a nameless, faceless servant who is clearly a picture of the invisible Holy Spirit. This servant also represents the many nameless, faceless people empowered by the Holy Spirit to act as friends of the bridegroom, sent by the Father to find, secure, and prepare a bride for His Son.

The servant (Holy Spirit) prepares and travels through the wilderness to find a bride for Isaac, the son, in obedience to Abraham (the Father). Isaac is a picture of Jesus, who is, in turn, the promised seed of Isaac. In fact, in Hebrews 11:18-19, Isaac is a type, shadow, and picture of Jesus: **"of whom it was said, 'In Isaac your seed shall be called,' concluding that God was able to raise him up, even from the dead, from which he also received him in a figurative sense."** Here, Scripture interprets Scripture and points to Isaac as a picture of Christ.

Rebekah is clearly the bride, the unmarried virgin. The faithful servant only says what the father, Abraham, tells him to say. In this way, he is a type or shadow of the Holy Spirit, whom Jesus said would only speak what He hears and bring to remembrance everything He said (see John 14:26, 16:13). The Holy Spirit also represents the prophetic that seeks out the people God is preparing in the wilderness, and that's exactly what this servant is doing. The father commissioned his servant to get a bride for his son, just as we go out and look for those who can become His bride.

The main focus of this type and shadow in Genesis 24 is the Holy Spirit's activity and responsibility to select, train, nurture, and prepare a bride. The second main focus is for the bride to marry the son. The bride's responsibility is to answer in voluntary love and willingly say, "Yes." She is to leave her family and all she has ever known and marry the son. The good news is we have read the back of the book, and the Holy Spirit succeeds! History will conclude with a bride that fills the heart of Jesus with joy and the Bible ends with the marriage supper of the Lamb.

THE HOLY SPIRIT IS THE SERVANT

The gospel story plays out throughout Genesis 24. It is the Father's eternal plan. Genesis 24:1 starts out, **"Now Abraham was old, well advanced in age."** Here, we see a picture of the Father, the Ancient of Days, in His eternal nature. The verse continues, **"and the Lord had blessed Abraham in all things."** The Ancient of Days possesses all things. We begin with the picture of God possessing everything. Genesis 24:2, **"So Abraham said to the oldest servant of the house, who ruled over all that he had,"** to go find a bride. This is clearly a type of the Holy Spirit who acts as an agent to execute the Father's will.

The Holy Spirit was also the agent who caused Mary to conceive. The angel told Joseph, **"for that which is conceived in her is of the Holy Spirit" (see Matthew 1:20).** God works through the Word and the Spirit. Jesus is the Word, the Holy Spirit is the Spirit, who is an agent and servant of the Father. Here, we see the triune Godhead acting out a story in the Old Testament and showing us the gospel narrative. The servant handled everything Abraham owned. It doesn't take much imagination to realize this servant represents the Holy Spirit. The Holy Spirit is the oldest, most faithful servant who rules over everything.

> **So Abraham said to the oldest servant of his house, who ruled over all that he had, "Please, put your hand under my thigh, and I will make you swear by the Lord, the God of heaven and the God of the earth, that you will not take a wife for my son from the daughters of the Canaanites, among whom I dwell; but you shall go to my country and to my family, and take a wife for my son Isaac." (Genesis 24:2)**

For the past two thousand years, the Holy Spirit has been going into all the world, to "faraway" countries, to find a wife for the Son. The servant was with Abraham from the beginning, just as the Holy Spirit was with the Father from the beginning. The servant knew Abraham's heart, just as the Holy Spirit knows the Father's heart (see Romans 8:27; 1 Corinthians 2:11). He was the only servant in Abraham's court who ruled over all of Abraham's business and was responsible for everything Abraham owned, just as the Holy Spirit is given this responsibility with the Father.

The friend of the bridegroom is also the friend of the bridegroom's ministry. In Matthew 9:15, Jesus gave this title to all twelve apostles: **"And Jesus said to them, 'Can the friends of the bridegroom mourn as long as the bridegroom is with them? But the days will come when the bridegroom will be taken away from them, and then they will fast.'"** They were part of the bride, but their main focus was to go to the ends of the earth (see Acts 1:8) to find a bride and awaken the bride's love for the Son of God. The apostles were also nameless, faceless ones, like the Holy Spirit.

Again, John 3:29 says, **"He who has the bride is the bridegroom; but the friend of the bridegroom, who stands and hears him, rejoices greatly because of the bridegroom's voice. Therefore this joy of mine is fulfilled."** The friend rejoices at the voice of the bridegroom. The prophetic is also about rejoicing to hear the bridegroom's voice for others, ourselves, our nations, our cities, and our families. Nothing excites us more than hearing the Father's voice and interpreting and applying it correctly. The friends of the bridegroom cannot mourn as long as the bridegroom is with them.

Paul said in 2 Corinthians 11:2, **"For I am jealous for you with godly jealousy. For I have betrothed you to one husband, that I may present you as a chaste virgin to Christ."** Paul's mandate was to present the church to Jesus Christ as a pure virgin, but they were getting off course. Paul, a friend of the bridegroom, betrothed them to Jesus Christ, so he did not want them to be seduced by the enemy or get off course. He had a passion and mandate to make them pure before Jesus. He did not write to the churches to grow his mailing list or to get more subscribers. As a friend of the bridegroom, he made sure they remained pure and preserved for the bridegroom.

The Holy Spirit is the ultimate friend and best man of the bridegroom. The Holy Spirit serves the Father's interests to secure a bride for His Son that will remain faithful through all eternity. The servant owned nothing himself yet had power over everything, just as the Holy Spirit speaks nothing of Himself yet has all power (see John 16:13; Acts 1:8).

Abraham told his servant, **"Go to my country and to my family."** Of course, the whole world belongs to God, so He said, "Go into all the world" (see Mark 16:15) and to "the whole family in heaven and earth" which will be "strengthened with might through His Spirit" (see Ephesians 3:15-16). Jesus also sent the Holy Spirit to the whole world to convict the world of sin, righteousness, and judgment (see John 16:7-8; Acts 1:8).

Isaac was a type of Christ who was offered up on Mount Moriah like Jesus was at Golgotha. There was even three days when Abraham thought he would have to kill Isaac, but the angel of the Lord stopped him, and a ram was provided—another picture of Jesus. Meanwhile, Abraham sacrificing his son was a picture of the Father sacrificing His Son. Abraham believed in receiving fresh daily manna and words from the mouth of God. If he didn't, he would have killed his son, through whose family line the Messiah would come.

SEARCHING FOR THE BRIDE

The father's heart and mission were clear: to go among the human race and God's family to find a wife for his son. He did not say, "Go among the angels and find a wife for my son." He said, "I don't want a bride from those Canaanite outsiders. I want a bride for my son from among my own family, the redeemed ones, so all the nations of the world can be blessed through the seed of Isaac and his bride. The seed of Isaac is Jesus. Jesus will come through the family line of Isaac and Rebekah, and He and His bride will possess everything because the Father possessed all things.

And the servant said to him, "Perhaps the woman will not be willing to follow me to this land. Must I take your son back to the land from which you came?" (Genesis 24:5). Here we see the Holy Spirit's commitment to God's plan. How many times have we taught a Bible study or preached or shared a message and thought, "Perhaps they won't hear or listen to me?"

> But Abraham said to him, "Beware that you do not take my son back there. The Lord God of heaven, who took me from my father's house and from the land of my family, and who spoke to me and swore to me, saying, 'To your descendants I give this land,' He will send His angel before you, and you shall take a wife for my son from there. And if the woman is not willing to follow you, then you will be released from this oath; only do not take my son back there." So the servant put his hand under the thigh of Abraham his master, and swore to him concerning this matter (Genesis 24:5-9).

"To your descendants I give this land" (Genesis 35:12). Abraham's descendants were given the land of Israel by God. The servant was not to take Isaac with him but would be freed from the responsibility if the woman would not follow. We are also freed of our responsibility if the called out ones do not respond to the call (see Ezekiel 3:19, 21). The woman must be willing to follow the Holy Spirit. That was the first requirement the Father made of the bride. The servant is freed from the responsibility if the woman will not follow, just as we are not responsible for those who do not give their lives to Jesus. The bridal company must say, "Yes," and be willing to follow the Holy Spirit. She must be prophetic and know what the Holy Spirit asks.

Truly following the Holy Spirit will cause us many problems and conflicts with our flesh. Like Rebekah, we must walk away from all we knew before we were saved. Sometimes even other believers will write us off for following the Holy Spirit. Many in the church are more interested in following tradition than following the Holy Spirit. The Holy Spirit will not leave the house until the bride is found, made ready, and comes. The Father will have a bride for His Son.

The Holy Spirit's search for a bride will succeed. God has sworn there will be a bride for His Son. The plan is foolproof. He will send angels and supernatural assistance reserved for this hour. Divine interventions and release of angelic ministries are guaranteed. The Father knows what He wants and will have a bride for His Son. He will use His divine power, the Holy Spirit, to bring it to pass.

If the woman is not willing to go, He will remove her candlestick (see Revelation 2:5). She must have oil in her lamp and her wick trimmed (Matthew 25:6-10). We must be willing to follow the Holy Spirit and see in the darkness. The bridegroom comes at midnight. If the woman is unwilling, then go find another bride. Here, man's free will enters the gospel story.

The bridegroom is coming for more than just a people, a Joel 2 army, a Hebrews 8 priesthood, and a Romans 8 sons and daughters. He is coming for His bride. This is God's highest agenda—to see a people who will love the Lord their God and love the Son with all their heart. History ends with the bridal supper of the Lamb. **"The Spirit and the bride say, 'Come!'" (see Revelation 22:17).**

The Holy Spirit arose with all His Master's goods at His disposal to adorn the bride of Christ, just as Eliezer readied Rebekah, the bride chosen for Abraham's son, Isaac. The Holy Spirit in Acts 2 was sent by God the Father to the earth (Acts 2:33). Christmas is the celebration of Jesus' first coming, but Pentecost is the celebration of the Holy Spirit's coming. Sometimes we try to explain away the mystery of one God in three expressions. It's not easy to explain the trinity, but we need to understand and behold the wonder of the mystery.

I Timothy 3:16 says, **"And without controversy great is the mystery of godliness: God was manifested in the flesh, justified in the Spirit, seen by angels, preached among the Gentiles, believed on in the world, received up in glory."** Jesus is now seated in glory, and all the Father's goods are at the Holy Spirit's disposal to adorn a bride for His Son.

THE BRIDE IS FOUND

Then the servant took ten of his master's camels and departed, for all his master's goods were in his hand. And he arose and went to Mesopotamia, to the city of Nahor. And he made his camels kneel down outside the city by a well of water at evening time, the time when women go out to draw water. Then he said, "O Lord God of my master Abraham, please give me success this day, and show kindness to my master Abraham. Behold, here I stand by the well of water, and the daughters of the men of the city are coming out to draw water. Now let it be that the young woman to whom I say, 'Please let down your pitcher that I may drink,' and she says, 'Drink, and I will also give your camels a drink'—let her be the one You have appointed for Your servant Isaac. And by this I will know that You have shown kindness to my master." (Genesis 24:10-14)

The servant had prayed, **"O Lord God of my master Abraham, please give me success this day."** We need to pray a similar prayer: "Lord, send Your power, not so we can say we had a good meeting but because we want Your people to love Your Son. Give us success. Help us, Father." That is the heart of the friends of the bridegroom. The prayer of Abraham's servant for success should be our prayer.

The servant needed ten camels to carry everything the Father had for the bride. This speaks of the abundance of God's gifts.

The camels carried abundant gifts and provisions to attract the bride and take her to meet her bridegroom.

Sometimes the Holy Spirit gives us the most intricate details of prophetic knowledge, and then it happens. Is God not watching over us, orchestrating all things? The gifts of the camels will convince her. The Holy Spirit gives us prophetic gifts: words of knowledge, words of wisdom, visions, dreams, discernment to make the vision plain, so we know what to look for. How many times has God given us prophetic revelation to know what He will do and what to look for?

The servant stopped in the evening, which today represents the close of this age. The camels will come in the evening—the last days—to convince the bride. The women were thirsty and drew water in the evening, representing the time when darkness covers the earth. As darkness covers the earth, people are thirsty, searching for something.

> **"And it shall come to pass in the last days, says God, that I will pour out of My Spirit on all flesh; your sons and your daughters shall prophesy, your young men shall see visions, your old men shall dream dreams. And on My menservants and on My maidservants I will pour out My Spirit in those days; and they shall prophesy. I will show wonders in heaven above and signs in the earth beneath: blood and fire and vapor of smoke" (Acts 2:17-19).**

All of God's power is at the Holy Spirit's disposal. My prayer is that God will send His power, and bring the camels so the people's hearts will be awakened with love!

Rebekah was a hard worker, willing to follow the Holy Spirit. She had an extravagant servant's heart to water the camels. God wants servants' hearts, not those looking out for themselves. We may fall short. We may not yet have a complete servant's heart, but we will not quit until we do. Just as the servant waited for the right bride, the Holy Spirit waits for the Father's perfect timing and orchestration. The well of water was where the thirsty would go. The Father is now waiting for the bride to go to the well and draw from His living water. The bride is a thirsty servant. When Rebekah was told the plan, she said, **"I will go" (see Genesis 24:58).** She did not make excuses and was willing to leave everything behind. She also worked hard to water the camels carrying the gifts and provisions. There is no telling how many buckets of water she filled and took to the ten camels. Camels can drink twenty gallons of water each, so it could have been about two hundred gallons!

Jesus' last pictures He gave to His disciples before the cross were also about serving before a wedding. His last parable was of the wedding. His last presentation of Himself was washing their feet with water and a servant's robe. God appears in the menial, like Rebekah pulling and carrying buckets of water as a servant. God often visits us during our most menial tasks, for instance when we visit the sick or mow the lawn.

A bondservant could be identified by a golden nose ring or bracelets. Gold represents the divine nature, which is also about servanthood, and gold bracelets on the wrists and hands also represent serving. Be a servant. This is the bridal call when the evening shadows fall. The "camels"—the gifts of the Holy Spirit —are coming! The prophetic servant says, "Lord, show me. Lead me to the person to whom I should direct my testimony to share Your love." This is the heart of the Father. This is the bridal call. This is what pastoring the prophetic is all about.

Here is an old hymn called "Camel Train," which summarizes the above interpretation:

Twas a day in early springtime,
By an ancient wayside well,

Eliezer paused to rest his camel train.
He had found a bride for Isaac
Ere the evening shadows fell,
For his weary journey had not been in vain.

Oh, get ready! Evening shadows fall.
Don't you hear the Eliezer call?
There's going to be a wedding,
And our joy will soon begin,
In the evening when the camel train comes in.

So he took the fair Rebekah,
Dressed in jewels rich and rare,
Quickly to her waiting bridegroom far away.
Where Rebekah loved her Isaac,
And he loved Rebekah fair;
Oh, it must have been a happy wedding day.

Now the blessed Holy Spirit,
From our Father God above,
Has come down to earth to find a worthy bride.
For our Isaac over yonder
Has prepared His tents of love,
And He wants His fair Rebekah by His side.

We have left our kinfolk gladly;
We have bade the world goodbye.
We've been called to be His pure and spotless bride;
Where we'll soon behold our Jesus
In that blest eternity.

"Lord, may we all develop our prophetic filters to hear and understand Your voice in these last days, so we can become faithful servants who seek and prepare Your beloved bride!"

DISCUSSION QUESTIONS

1. Name some of the ways John the Baptist was "the friend of the bridegroom."

2. In your own words, explain the friend of the bridegroom's role in Hebrew culture.

3. What is the correlation between the spirit of Elijah, John the Baptist, and the end-times forerunners ministry? Explain. (see Isaiah 40:3-5; Malachi 4:5-6; John 1:23)

4. What are the three levels of interpreting Scripture, as described in this chapter? Why should we desire to achieve the highest level of interpretation?

5. Based on the interpretive story of Isaac and Rebekah in Genesis 28, who does Abraham represent?

6. Who does Abraham's servant, believed to be Eliezer, represent? Describe some of the similarities between Eliezer (the type, shadow, and picture) and the real.

7. What do the ten camels in this story represent? What interpretive purpose do they serve?

8. Who does Rebekah represent? What are Rebekah's characteristics? Why are these important today?

9. What was Rebekah's first requirement? What does this mean for the church?

10. In your own words, what is the Father's heart in this story? What is the bridal call?

MORNINGSTAR
SCHOOL OF THE PROPHETS

MorningStar School of the Prophets is a monthly, weekend intensive experience designed to equip you to walk in your prophetic calling.

Learn to hear God's voice, grow in your gifts, and be released into your calling with in-depth teaching and training from Chris Reed, the MorningStar team, and special guest speakers.

This special program happens one weekend every month from September through May and is available online or in-person.

**Learn more and enroll today
at: www.MSSOP.com**

Give God your gap year and reap the benefits for life.

Join us this coming school year and find your place in the next move of God! Receive in-depth teaching, training, and mentoring in supernatural ministry. We offer one-year ministry certificate programs as well as associate and bachelor degrees with five different majors from which to choose. Our high-impact programs include the Company of Prophets, the School of Worship, Special Forces Missions, the School of Communications, and the School of Revival.

Learn more at: mstaru.com

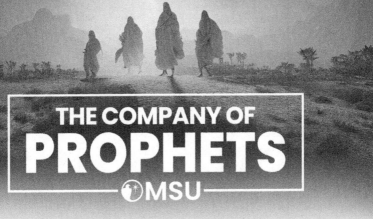

THE COMPANY OF
PROPHETS
⏀MSU

The MorningStar University Company of Prophets is a full-time academic major providing in-depth teaching, training, and mentoring in all aspects of the prophetic ministry within the context of a healthy prophetic community.

Drawing from MorningStar Ministries' three decades of prophetic ministry experience, the MSU Company of Prophets trains students in three key aspects of prophetic ministry: living a prophetic lifestyle modeled after Christ's life, effective interpersonal prophetic ministry, and prophetic watchman ministry.

If you're looking to grow in your walk with God, build strong relationships with others, and develop your prophetic gift to the next level, we are here to be your launchpad.

Scan the QR code to apply now or visit MStarU.com to learn more.

Made in the USA
Monee, IL
07 April 2024

56531853R00148